IF I CAN BE HONEST

Selected Prose from the Four Years of *Autofocus Lit* (2020-2024)

edited by
Michael Wheaton

Autofocus Books
Easton, Pennsylvania

Published by Autofocus Books
autofocusbooks.com

Anthology/Literature
ISBN: 978-1-957392-44-8

Cover design by Amy Wheaton
Library of Congress Control Number: 2025937411

IF I CAN BE HONEST

Table of Contents

Heartbreak

The Body

Violence

Death

Life

Introduction

Michael Wheaton

A few months ago, I paid a sum I will not disclose, and that Chase Bank is still covering at an interest rate of 18.99%, to split an eight-foot sales table at the Portland Book Festival. I sold enough books to make it fun, but travel was steep, and if I was smart about money, I wouldn't have started a small press. I was there, mostly, to see friends.

At these functions, I say so many unconsidered words that I rarely remember the details of most conversations. At this one, though, I remember an insignificant detail I overheard from a conversation I had just left so I could chat up a visitor drawn into the display of books. It was a comment from Mike Nagel, who wrote the first book I ever published, talking to Kristine Langley Mahler, the director of Split/Lip Press who shared the table, and whose own book was on my side of it. "I love introductions to books," Mike said. "I would read a book of just introductions to books." He said it in his kind of joking manner that is completely serious. Or in his complete seriousness that he sort of manners with jokes. (Perhaps that is me.) But I had, by the time of the PDX Book Fest, begun to compile this anthology.

When I returned to the conversation, it had moved on. I stared into the museum's high ceiling and planned to write an introduction to this book so good that someone might one day place it in an anthology like that, because I'm unable to do anything half decent in life or art without impossible standards for what I don't yet know I am doing.

This introduction, as you may consider three paragraphs in, is not that introduction. I made some notes for that introduction the following month when I was on a couch in the house that my family and I are renting in eastern Pennsylvania (six months post-move from Central Florida), listening to a seventy-year-old tube radio I had bought weeks earlier for a number I will disclose ($84) from an antique store we found in the center of town.

The notes, basically, prompted me to make a half-baked metaphor between direct one-way non-digital communication in radio and books and their superiority over the social media apps that I hate how much I seem to love and that, in 2020, were largely the vehicles with which I started the online journal this anthology memorializes. That was another part of the notes. I would go into what was going on with me, other than wanting to become a book editor and make friends, when I decided to start the journal, then podcast, then press.

But that's not what a good introduction does. The most important thing, I think, is to not overstay its welcome. Give context only for the contents inside, the processes undergone to arrive at its final form. I'll use this opportunity to say that making decisions for this book wasn't easy. The journal published 318 pieces over four years. I had to make rules to give myself constraints. Otherwise, I must admit I don't know what I'm doing.

Now I should tell you the rules:

No poetry. Nothing longer than 3,000 words. No more than seven sections. Each section, no more than seven pieces, no less than five, and no more than 8,000 words. Nothing with accompanying images, and nothing that I published as a review. Use short, medium, and longer length pieces of varied approach, tone, or form in each section. Use a mix of pieces from 2020 – 2024 throughout the book (and as many years possible in each section). Include Autofocus Books authors who I formed editorial relationships with due to their *Autofocus Lit* piece, but avoid, when possible, collecting pieces already in existing Autofocus books.

Despite never once in my life reading an anthology in a way that wasn't guided by the table of contents, and therefore discontinuous, uneven, incomplete, and intermittent, I wanted each section to make a one-sitting read and the book to make an enjoyable emotional arc over time. The end of each section should lead thematically to the beginning of the next. The total word count should be less than 55,000 words. Which means I don't have much more room to spare here. But, if I can be honest, I broke a couple of rules when I thought it suited the book. Breaking rules is important to making something interesting.

I wrote the phrase "if I can be honest" in the previous paragraph because I named this book while selecting pieces, and using it here seems right. Drafting, I wrote just "honestly," which I didn't need either. I changed it to "to be honest" to no real effect before remembering my working title. The only reason to keep an extra phrase there is with the complication of if I can. Because that's why I started the journal, and why I'm having a hard time writing this introduction, aside from my outlandish expectations for it. Most of the time, I can't. I am trying to control other people's perceptions of me, despite only guessing at how I'm seen or heard.

I may seem honest now, but that's because I realized an introduction to a book called *If I Can Be Honest* should feel really honest. Four years of editing this online journal and talking on a podcast, several years of working on other writers' personal books, and five years of failing to write some of my own, has made it easier to reveal to others the way I see myself and the world. It's always been easier on the page, alone. Readers seem distant enough. I can craft it later. But face-to-face, it's only become easier with strangers. If the truth gets too hard for me in my main relationships, I lie. Or withhold, which is safer. I used to think I was protecting the other person, but mainly I want to be safe from the consequence of being myself to someone else.

When I imagined the first path for this essay, to win the hypothetical admiration of a writer who would hypothetically select it for a hypothetical anthology, I wanted the writing to feel like art instead of information. But I had to pivot from the original idea with the radio because

I realized the essay was doomed by the fact that I thought, inaccurately, that I had something to say. The truth must surprise. Then, in revision, it must be controlled. Through compression and form, I must attempt to reconsider the material into a surprise for the reader. Artifice required. But just enough. Real honesty, perhaps, is most important in the slight untruths rendered in service of narrative and thematic convenience.

I surprised myself while drafting this introduction when I realized I was lying about something, and not in this service. Or I was withholding. I claimed that I made rules for selecting pieces in this anthology simply to make choices easier. That thought was secondary. My primary thought was that I needed an easy administrative shorthand in situations where I had to explain to writers-who-have-since-become-friends why I didn't recollect their piece here in print, when it costs money and when I did it for forty-three other people, in a way that they would still like me. If I can be generous, I would say my insecurity is based on empathy. I don't want a writer to think less of their work because of my decision. I know they will not like as much as I do some of the pieces in here instead. But my insecurity is not empathy. I am projecting the assumption that most people are as weak as I am.

Even now, the work on this anthology complete, I worry mostly about how my selections reflect on me. The rules may be read in ways I don't foresee. You may have seen right through them and noticed ones I should have made based on your value system and what you assume of mine. Perhaps, if rules were important, I would have made one about writing a shorter introduction. I wouldn't have declared that I broke some. I wouldn't have back-formed others for justification. I would have included the couple of rules I didn't mention.

Otherwise, I am grateful to publish this anthology without someone else's permission, funding, or timeline. I think I'll like having a physical object with a representative sample of a thing that only existed digitally. Incomplete but tangible proof for the future. I found this book's seven sections (Friends, Family, Heartbreak, The Body, Violence, Death, and

Life) to be the biggest thematic containers for the writing that the journal published during its four years. Many pieces could fit into several. There used to be a section called "Education," made of six pieces (mostly now cut) set in classrooms, but that theme turned out to be, not a container like the others, but a related component for any of the seven. But can you even believe me anymore? If it matters enough, you'd have to trust my motives. I have overstayed my welcome.

The dates at the end of each piece in this anthology are original publication dates, ignoring the exact day. Time hazes the importance of such things. Or that is my choice. The date below this line, however, is a generalized period that contained the writing of this introduction.

February 2025

FRIENDS

D.T. Only Reads My Stuff If It's Really Short Because He's a Baby with a Wife and Kids and Adult Responsibilities Blah Blah Blah

Aaron Burch

My buddy, Kevin, texts me and our other buddy, D.T., that he's feeling a surge of hope and healing coming his way.

D.T. texts us that he's thinking of applying to a job, that he's hitting the point where he hates what he does.

I text them that I don't know how long I can keep this up, but I'm feeling especially inspired and productive and like a new me.

*

I go on a run and TV on the Radio sing:

Oh, I keep telling myself
'Don't worry, be happy'
Oh, you keep telling yourself
'Everything's gonna be okay'

*

I text Kevin and D.T. to don't worry, be happy.

D.T. texts, Like that annoying dumbass song from the 80s?

Kevin texts, Didn't you write an essay about that song?

I text back, Actually, yeah, but I was quoting TV on the Radio not Bobby McFerrin. But maybe they were quoting Bobby McFerrin?

Kevin texts, Probably.

D.T. texts, Dumbass.

I text back that everything's gonna be okay.

*

I read this excerpt from a Joy Williams short story:

"You're a Christian, right? I bet, I mean, I can imagine it."

"I believe in guilt and longing," Liberty admitted. "Confession and continual defeat. The circle and the spiral."

*

D.T. texts that he needs a fucking break from… life.

Kevin texts back that life doesn't allow breaks for artists.

I text back that I am currently taking a break from life, and that I recommend it.

*

I go on another run and TV on the Radio sing:

Rain comes down like it always does
This time, I've got seeds on ground.

*

I text my buddy, Kevin, and our other buddy, D.T., asking if they'll read a new short thing I wrote.

D.T. texts back, How many words? I only have time for a certain number of words.

I text, 400.

D.T. texts, I have time for that.

D.T. reads the story. Really good ending, he texts.

Kevin doesn't text anything. Maybe he's busy, in the middle of a surge of hope and healing.

*

I go on a run and think about circles and spirals, and guilt and longing, confession and continual defeat.

*

Kevin texts that he was busy but that he liked the story.

D.T. texts that he has officially applied to the job he told us about.

I text that I finished another new story and ask if they want to read it. I tell them it is about guilt and longing and confession and continual defeat.

Kevin texts, YES.

D.T. texts back, I don't know if I'll have time today but send it anyway.

I text back that this one is closer to 750 words.

Kevin texts that maybe I could cut it to 500 words.

I text back that I knew when finishing it that it was probably more words than D.T. would have time for.

Kevin texts a long, dumb, jokey title, the idea being that it might get D.T.'s attention and make him want to read it.

*

I go on more runs; I listen to more songs; Kevin and D.T. and I text each other about hope and healing, about inspiration and productivity, about needing breaks and taking breaks, about life being circles and spirals; I read more stories with excerpts that grab my attention; I see in everything—in runs and songs and texts and stories and friends and life—potential and beauty, a wealth of seeds on ground; I write more stories; I write this story; I send this story to Kevin and D.T.; I send this story to you.

May 2024

[Lonely Anywhere]

Nina Perlman

I used to stalk the Facebook pages of people like whom I most aspired to be. Scouring their lists of favorite books and movies and musicians, I fell deeper, desperately—I knew these were the kinds of things that made a person.

Freshman year of college, I met a girl named Sarah in my Darkroom Photo II class. She was in the year above me, a slim, shy girl from Tennessee, who wore red Dansko clogs in the lab, slipping them on and off her feet as she processed her negatives, or looked at them through a loop against the light table. She listened to The Everybodyfields, an indie folk/alt-country band from nearby her hometown in Tennessee. The band was co-founded and fronted by Sam Quinn and Jill Andrews, who met in 1999 while working at a summer camp.

In the summer of 2007, at a sleep-away camp in upstate New York that I had been attending for five years, I met a guy named Jonah. It was his first and last summer in attendance. He was a junior counselor, and I was a "super senior," fifteen when he must have been eighteen.

I bought three albums by The Everybodyfields on iTunes—the only albums they released before splitting up, an all-too-common consequence of forming a band with your significant other. I listened on my headphones in the darkroom, turning on the enlarger for two seconds at a time, another two seconds, and again, moving the mat board at each interval, a test to determine the correct exposure time for a particular negative. I assumed Sarah was listening to the same songs as I watched her move her photos from the stop bath to the fix, then walk her tray from the red light of the darkroom to the incandescent outer lab to check her print. I don't remember anything else, any other favorite books or shows or music from her profile.

When I make lists, I never cross things off. I simply turn the page and make a new one, including all the tasks never accomplished from the days before. A rotating replenishment of things that must be said. When Jonah messaged me on Facebook out of the blue four years later, the same fall semester that I took a photo class with a slim girl in red Danskos, I imagined a life with him. On The Everybodyfields' 2005 album *Plague of Dreams,* there's a song called "By Your Side." I belt it in the dorm shower.

I still get pretty nostalgic about camp, he told me. *There was just something about that whole experience that was so perfect and wonderful. I would really like to go back, but I'm not sure if trying to recreate that same experience would be a good idea or not. It's just something I think about often.* He had recently graduated from college and bought himself a one-way ticket to Portland. His family was from the Northeast, *which, as you know, is kind of industrial in nature. But you go out to the northwest and it's all so green and the air feels so much cleaner, and there's a lot more of a push for an active lifestyle. Everyone is about outdoor activities and riding bikes and I feel like I'd be really comfortable there. That and I feel like there are all these little signs that tell me that's where I should be, that that's where I'd thrive. I'm just following my instincts and seeing how I like it.*

The Everybodyfields' music has a kind of country-leaning vibe that I've been told is unexpected of me, but which reminds me of summers looking up at the stars in Hilton Head—a brief respite from the near-empty sky I'm used to, a new perspective, a new sense of where I stand in context—of a kind of storytelling like in Broadway musicals, of singing "Golden Slumbers" with Jonah at the picnic tables while he played guitar, a rehearsal for a visiting day performance. Nothing romantic ever happened between us, no encounters beyond those few brief rehearsals at the picnic tables and two performances onstage, but I remember him with a kind of warmth granted to someone who once loved you, who you trust always will.

Nostalgia's a deceiving thing, I wrote back. *You think it's about what was happening, but it's really about how you felt.* For five days we messaged back and forth. Re-reading now, I see myself yearning to escape the city, to surround myself in nature, *like when the grass is long enough that you can just feel it coming up all around your body as you lay on your back. I always pass those sorts of places when I take the train: farms or fields or similar spots where they just stuck some train tracks but seem to have left the surrounding area untouched.* I don't recognize this version of myself, expressing these desires most likely adopted to match what I saw in him and reflected back. *There's also the stars: only on incredibly rare occasions have I ever seen a sky full of stars. I saw them at camp, I may see them on vacations or something, depending where I go, but on a regular basis, the sky is lacking, and I am literally left every night staring at the sky, enjoying the phenomenon where you can faintly see a couple stars wayyy up by staring harder into the blackness of the sky. Was that explanation clear enough to understand? I don't know what kinds of skies you regularly see.*

Sarah made collages, combining her own photographs with images she found in vintage magazines or postcards. She installed them in the corner of the classroom, one image folded in half exactly where the walls met. Once, alone in the computer lab, playing a song from The Everybodyfields' 2004 album *Halfway There: Electricity and the South,* Sarah walked in. She asked how I'd heard about the Everybodyfields—they were a local band from her hometown—and I told her a friend of mine had recommended them. The Everybodyfields' final album is titled *Nothing is Okay.* The ninth song on the album is titled "Everything is Okay."

Perhaps the point isn't to recreate a past experience that once left you feeling wonderful, I told Jonah, *but to look around for opportunities to find the feeling again. Where you'll find it now will likely be different than before, because you're a different version of yourself, and you're looking for different things.* I've listened in the middle of the night, in the yellow light of bedrooms in Baltimore, in Paris, in Berlin, and in my mother's apartment. When I could still hear my roommates chatting on the couch, but I couldn't hear the music anymore because it had been playing on a loop and I'd completely tuned it out, fading into the background until I shut my laptop and heard an unexpected silence. I wish for the allowance to express things without words, or where the words I have aren't quite the ones I need. To communicate through listening.

Around the same time, I decided I would learn to speak Esperanto, a *universal language* composed of recognizable bits and pieces from other western languages, constructed to be fair in its small points of entry for anyone who wanted to learn it. But Esperanto is actually spoken by very few, so rather than being equally understandable to all, Esperanto is just equally ambiguous. Speaking Esperanto, I'd be an equal distance from everyone. Still, I started to learn more about it. I used Google to translate quotes from artists I admired into Esperanto and posted them on Tumblr. I wrote vocabulary words into my notebooks. I titled projects in Esperanto, which saved me the struggle of coming up with titles that carried the right meaning. I joked about the effort I was exerting to learn a language no one else would understand, that I was building myself a void in which to shout. But this goal somehow felt safer than the way I had been operating. Sometimes, when the failure to connect to another person feels particularly devastating, or the risk of this failure looms particularly large, I wish that I could point to something aside from myself, identifying *that thing* as the wall between us. The other person in a conversation feels far away because they don't speak my language. If mine is universal, but they still don't understand, at least I made my best attempt. I signed up for a free Esperanto program online. I emailed my Lesson 1 exercises to the instructor. I never followed-up, waiting for his response. He sent me my corrections a year later.

I posted on my Tumblr, that early endless-scrolling void, *Are you still reading this?* Within minutes Jonah replied, *Yes.*

May 2023

A Field of Telephones

Zach Savich

The new friend asks me to tell her something about myself that she doesn't know. I was never a kid who could say their favorite color. I liked colors. I told the teacher I wasn't sure when blue became green. She had me tested for color blindness. Once, I misread *birding* as *braiding.* The branches wove.

*

I hadn't been asked a question like that in a minute. There's the idea that your life story starts when something happens that you'd need to mention before you could say anything else. There's the other idea that your life story starts after the above has passed and you could start your story anywhere. I'm interested in the story after and around the story we "need to tell."

*

Jack Gilbert: "What I'm interested in is writing about people who have gotten beyond the beginning." (Yet also: we ask of each sentence, could this be, at last, our final, eventual beginning, however late or untoward?)

*

Or: I don't need to tell you where I've been, for us to be here, but we can talk if you want.

*

I said I was working on a study of the poet Theodore Roethke (1908-1963). I was about to go to Saginaw, Michigan, his hometown. Isn't there a song about Saginaw, the other new friend said. Lefty Frizzel's "Saginaw." 1964. We were waiting on the pretzel bites. She began to sing: "I was born in Saginaw, Michigan. I grew up in a house on Saginaw Bay."

*

For a long time, the story I needed to tell before saying anything else was cancer. My thirties. I often didn't need to tell it. It was obvious. I got used to people in public asking if I was all right. The palliative doctor asked what I wanted. "Moments," I said.

*

The person who says they want "moments" knows they may have only "moments" left. Sun on my wrist one afternoon I could handle it, among treatments. I preferred the light when it steadily flared.

*

I was born a bit southeast of Saginaw. The house was sunflowers taller than anyone. I saw a stranger peeing in the raspberries.

*

Sun tea on a stone. Potato bugs under.

*

Johnny Cash covers Frizzel's "Saginaw." A mix of hard-scrabble and schmaltz: very Roethke. Consider the beginning of his poem "The Saginaw Song":

In Saginaw, in Saginaw,

The wind blows up your feet,
When the ladies' guild puts on a feed
There's beans on every plate.

*

The palliative doctor was a few years ago. The few-years-ago tumor was in a scar from an earlier tumor, or was in the scar from a tumor from before that. A confusing metaphor, redundant. "You can't punch yourself in the same tumor twice," a friend said.

*

The rhymes above are slick. Neither "feed" nor "plate" rhymes with "feet," not exactly. But each picks up part of the sound. Their chime with "feet," therefore, is more ambient. An overtone that emerges from plucking the string of "feed" and the string of "plate." The rhyme with "feet" isn't a single harmony, it's a harmonic.

*

The harmonic, which emerges within and exceeds.

*

Rhyme is not a matching game. It arranges, activates, assembles. And, in the next two lines, shifts, settles: "And if you eat more than you should, / Destruction is complete." We end with a resolution, "complete" calling back to "feet," fulfilling the ambient effect generated by "feet / feed / plate." Resolving the imperfect matching. Meanwhile, "should," in calling back to the "d" in "feed," establishes a counterchord, an undertone, with dissonance: "complete / feed" echoing through "feet / feed / should." Rhyme is in motion.

*

Forms of language are forms of thought, as we often said. Ways of swimming. You don't need to use them, but you'll use them, in ways, in particular waters. And everyone who used them, who really used them, or who I want to say really used them, really needed to swim. There's no language without it, just as there's no swimming without the body. Even in stillness, the body is moving. In the silentest reading. You can't move any part without moving everywhere. Reeds in the shallows and mixing the colder depths and the warm algae.

*

"I don't want you to have to find my body," I said to my wife, during those years of moments. "I can find your body," she said.

*

Hard-scrabble, schmaltz: this was the landscape, childhood. In Saginaw, Roethke receives a postcard from his cousin, in 1916. It shows a macaroni factory ("last year Larkin customers received more than 1,000,000 packages of macaroni"). "Dear Theodore," the message reads. "We are just going through this factory. It is very large."

*

Another, from the cousin on a visit to Detroit, sweetly: "Hello Theodore. How do you feel after your picnic?" And here's one from his father, in 1918, a few years before the father's death. "We are all having a good time and I shot a deer the first day in the woods be a good boy and help Mama all you can Papa."

*

The father's death defined his life. He didn't return to Saginaw when his mother was dying.

*

A landscape, childhood. His father's greenhouses, 25 acres. Up in the night to fiddle the steam. Visible from his bedroom window, immortal diamond. "It was a jungle, and it was paradise," he wrote. In the present, shards of glass sometimes work their way up in neighbors' gardens.

*

Shards of glass working their moments up in neighbors' gardens. This is the legacy, the university.

*

Father and uncle ran the business. Largest florist in Michigan. Manure and roses. Lived next door to it and each other. Then the business went bad and the uncle killed himself and the father died from cancer and the poet wore a long black coat for years. "Carnations, verbenas, cosmos."

*

Our garden was a little strip. Even the smallest strip can be garden. Fecund glitch. From my bedroom, I could see the tree with snowball blossoms. Put one down your pants. Bare room, wood. Light I have seen a few times since.

*

I asked my friend the attorney, "What advice would you give me for finding an attorney, in case it helps with dying?" "My advice is, I will be your attorney," he said.

*

In the archives at the University of Washington, in Seattle, among the postcards and other items of Roethke's childhood, there's a set of collectible cards that recall the more saccharine, jaunty moments from his poems, especially in his lighter pieces and poems for children. One shows a dopey, grinning kid whittling near a windmill. "De happiness off my heart sprouts oudt off my face," it says. Another shows a boy and a dog: "If I had viskers like dis feller's I vunder vould I be somebody's pet." Another: "The moon in the sky is a custard pie."

*

"I had a Donkey, that was all right, / But he always wanted to fly my Kite," begins his poem, "The Donkey." Sensibility oh la.

*

I surrendered my pens, sanitized my hands. I told the librarian that I was a scholar of materiality who interpreted biographical effects, authors' notebooks, and other physical ephemera as sculptural artifacts. I needed to touch the stuff, bypass the microfiche. So held a lock of his childhood hair up to my ear. "Theodore's first haircut."

*

After which my notes digressed into a shaggy meditation on Keats' poem about a lock of Milton's hair. Cut it.

*

And put on his glasses. Opened the cigarette case that had been in his pocket when he died, swimming in a pool outside Seattle. Counted the cigarettes in it, strained for a lyrical thought: *These would have become his breath.* Blew a small whistle. Keys he stole from hotels.

*

Is heritage lineage? Or an echoing span. This shaking that speaks through us. In which meaning is. Or in which meaning is released.

*

The librarian, interested that I was a poet, told me he'd been friendly with Elizabeth Bishop when she briefly taught there, shortly after Roethke's death. They once went for a drive. She said a field of flowers looked like a field of telephones.

January 2024

The Gravity of the Situation

Mike Nagel

The dog is seriously not okay with the squirrels in this neighborhood. I get the feeling he thinks J and I don't fully appreciate the danger we're all in. I have to admit that these squirrels do seem like they're up to something. A re-arrangement of our neighborhood's natural resources. They're taking nuts from over here and putting them over there. It's a massive undertaking. Ambitious in scale and scope.

I looked it up. One oak tree can drop ten thousand acorns a year. There must be a dozen oak trees on my street alone. There's one in my front yard. It's dropping acorns right now. One every couple of minutes. They roll down the roof and into the gutter, then down the gutter and into the yard like some sort of unimpressive Rube Goldberg machine.

The squirrels have their work cut out for them and they're uniquely unqualified to do it. I read that squirrels forget where they bury 90% of their stash. They bury a nut, then immediately forget where they buried that nut.

"Oh crap," they think. "Here we go again."

*

I ran into my neighbor Curtis the other day. He was sweeping his front lawn with a broom.

"Curtis, are you sweeping your front lawn with a broom?" I said. "Because that's what it looks like."

It was the acorns, he said. In the morning, he goes out to get the paper, and he's always stepping on acorns. It's painful. "Like stepping on Legos," he says. He's bagging them up and sending them off to the dump where they can't hurt anybody anymore. He's filled three bags already. He's working on bag number four.

"I hear you," I said, "but we can't go losing our heads out here. That's exactly what the acorns *want* us to do."

I saw a TED Talk where this guy said that, over thousands of years, trees manipulated humans into spreading their seeds across the planet. We did all the hard work for them. They made us think it was our idea.

*

"Life, uh, finds a way," Jeff Goldblum says in *Jurassic Park*. But I think what he means is: *Life always finds a sucker.*

*

Back in the living room, the dog and I are pressing our faces against the window with our eyes the size of Frisbees. The squirrels are at it again this morning. They don't seem to know what they're doing, but they're doing it with the blind enthusiasm required to achieve any great undertaking. They just might pull it off, whatever it is.

If you're not picky about the outcome, a lot of possibilities open up to you in terms of how to accomplish it.

See: John Cage's stochastic discography

See: Evolutionary theory

See: The whole goddam universe for that matter

There is no method to this madness.

Madness *is* the method.

*

"I'll play it," Miles Davis said to Bob Weinstock before recording *If I Were a Bell,* "and tell you what it is later."

*

For a long time, I didn't realize we even *had* an oak tree in our front yard. Apparently these things are really easy to overlook even when they're full grown, the size of a two story building. We'd been living here for months when our neighbor rang our doorbell and asked if she could hang her son's piñata from our tree.

I said, "We have a tree?"

By next year, we should have ten thousand of them.

The year after that: one hundred million.

That day, I stood in my front yard with my new neighbor, watching kids in party hats whack the shit out of some rainbow-colored goat, the plastic-wrapped hard candies flying all over the place, catching the sun like stained glass.

Later, I started finding candy in the bushes.

*

Now in the mornings, the dog and I get up early and sit at the window while J sleeps in the other room. She doesn't fully appreciate the danger we're all in. We try not to bother her with it. I drink coffee and play Miles Davis quietly out of my laptop speakers. The classics, mainly. *The Birth of Cool. Relaxin' with the Miles Davis Quintet,* featuring the upbeat Frank Loesser tune "If I Were a Bell," which quickly became a Miles Davis classic.

He played it, I think. *But did he ever tell us what it was?*

"It's important to stay cool," I remind the dog. "It's important to stay relaxed."

The squirrels are staying cool. They're staying relaxed. They're putting on weight, and it's going straight to their hips. By January they're each twenty pounds, waddling around the yards with their arms full of acorns. They're doing Curtis' work for him. They're moving the acorns from his yard into my yard. And they're moving the acorns from my yard into his. The old switcheroo. They're taking their time and really doing it right.

This morning, I swear I saw one heading over to Curtis' with its arms full of Gobstoppers and a Jolly Rancher in its mouth.

April 2021

My Friends

David Schuman

I fell in love with a woman in college who later became my friend. At the end of sophomore year, there were a few nights in her apartment when we made out. At one point, I pulled off my T-shirt, and she slipped it back over my head, guided my arms through the sleeves as my mother had when I was small. Then she went home for the summer, and I stayed in Philadelphia working at Domino's on South Street delivering pizzas on my bike. I kept a thick rubber band around my wrist. I'd be out riding around with a pizza strapped to the back of my bike, the city whooshing past my cheeks, and every time I thought of the woman I loved, I'd pull the elastic and let it snap hard into the flesh of my wrist. By the end of the summer, I had a raised welt across the tender skin inside my wrist. Those few months, I never even spoke to the woman on the phone. When she came back to school, she started dating a boy named Xander. I understood that it would be difficult to compete with a name like that. Anyway, I had sort of moved on. But she and I became very good friends. In fact, she introduced me to my wife.

I have a friend who had a difficult divorce, then a new relationship that he ended with some amount of regret because the woman was quite a bit younger than he was and her parents refused to accept him. This was followed by a brief second marriage and then another divorce. At the end of all that, he had terrible back pain accompanied by leg numbness, and no doctor seemed to be able to help. The summer after his second divorce, I invited him on our family vacation in the Outer Banks. *The ocean might be good for your back,* I said. The way it turned out, he and I drove from New Jersey together and met my wife and her family, who were already down there. It was such a fun drive. We made each other laugh the way we always had. The car smelled like salami because we'd stopped at an Italian grocery on the way out of Jersey so that we could make an antipasto with dinner that night. On the Chesapeake Bay Bridge, I pointed out the osprey nests. I felt like a real friend, doing my friend some good in his sad time. When we arrived at the beach, my friend and I prepared an amazing meal for my wife and her mom and stepfather. We ate out on the deck with a view of the sun setting over the sound, pelicans flying over in loose Vs. Pasta, bread, wine, everything. It seemed like the cloud of unhappiness over my friend was dissipating. We all got drunk and had a great time. But when I went up to bed and got in next to my wife, she said, *I don't know why you brought him here.*

Sometimes I say to my daughter, *You're my daughter, but you're also my best friend.* My daughter does not want me to be her best friend. She's twelve. She wants friends who are her age and who are girls and not middle-aged men. The truth is, I don't want to be best friends with her either. Being best friends with her would mean I'd have to watch a lot of YouTube videos.

In third grade, my best friend moved to New Mexico, and though we promised to remain best friends, we lost touch after a few letters. I remember that one of his letters had a drawing of a New Mexican lizard and, above it in careful block letters, the word HERPATOLOGIST, which is what he'd decided to become. I was jealous. We didn't have lizards in New Jersey. Decades later, I discovered that my friend had actually become a writer, and that he worked for a creative writing program at a university, just like me. I found this out when I saw his name as the winner of a prize named after one of my favorite writers, Donald Barthelme, for a short story he'd written about Taylor Swift. The prize was one I'd fantasized about winning. A few years after that, I ran into him at a writing program convention in Chicago. He remembered me from the old days in East Windsor. *Both of us turning out writers,* I said. *Must have been something in the water.* My friend looked at me like he didn't think we'd drunk the same water at all. He excused himself and went to talk to some important people. I teach his story still, in my microfiction class. I don't have hard feelings about this friend.

I have a friend who is a pretty famous poet. She lives in a rambling apartment filled with beautiful and whimsical objects. There is nothing in her place that you would not want to pick up and inspect. But much is delicate, not unlike my friend herself, who is tiny and sometimes wears red shoes like an elf. In her apartment are antique puppets that, if you stuck your hand inside them, might fall apart. This friend of mine suffers from health problems that make her high risk during this pandemic. She has barely ventured out in seven months, and our visits, our wine nights, have been mostly virtual since last March, except for one evening recently when we met up on her apartment building's roof overlooking the park. We slipped crackers underneath our masks to nibble, sipped our wine through straws. My friend loves a coconut cake that is only available in one store in the city. The cake comes in a small white box bound in red and white twine. When unpacked, it resembles an even smaller white box, furred with coconut flakes. The slice my friend serves herself is the size of slice you would present to a doll. My friend has written poems about dolls. She has also written poems so sad that they make my mother, an unsentimental woman, weep. After we eat our cake on the roof, it's time for me to go. My friend is always apologizing about keeping me from other things I might want to be doing, like spending time with my family. This makes me sad. *Believe me,* I tell her. *I spend plenty of time with them. Too much time, these days,* I say. But the fact is it's getting late, and I do need to get home because I want to watch a home-organizing show on Netflix with my wife.

A friend has commissioned a local metal worker to make a gate in her alley which will prevent trespassers but will also be beautiful. My friend asks if I'll help select the color scheme for the gate. My friend has made several mockups of a portion of the gate and painted them in the combinations of colors she is most interested in. The mockups, made of foam core and painted with precision, look like they must have taken my friend hours and hours to make. I stand in the alley and my friend holds one mockup up, then puts it down, then holds up another. The colors are tasteful mossy greens and earth tones. They all look good against the red brick. I ask her to hold each mockup up again as I step backward and forward, squinting, trying to look like the painting student I once was. I decide on the mockup with the dark green and ochre combination. A week later, my friend texts. The metal worker has installed the finished gate in her alley, and she isn't crazy about the colors. She isn't blaming me, per se, but texts that at full-size the colors look a bit "institutional." *It was probably my mockups*, she says. I drive over to her place to see the gate for myself. My friend is standing in front of her house, looking at it. It's a very tall, heavy gate, with the bars painted dark green and some larger planes in ochre as we'd decided. I try to reassure her, since the impressive gate looks like something she'll be living with for a very long time. *I don't think it looks institutional at all,* I say. But then her housemate comes through the alley from the back, grips the bars, and tries to rattle. The gate is so heavy there is no sound. *Let me out, Warden,* my friend's housemate says.

In eighth or ninth grade, a friend spent an entire evening trying to convince me to jerk him off. I was sleeping over at his house, in the living room, our two sleeping bags laid out in front of the television. His family had a big-screen television in the days when not many families did. His father worked on Wall Street. His father had a white Mercedes convertible in the garage that nobody ever drove. We had a plan that once we got our licenses, we would drive the Mercedes to Seaside with the top down. My friend told me that he could jerk me off, too. After I did him. Or he could do me first. He was really nonchalant about it, but I could tell he had rehearsed it in his head. I can't say I wasn't intrigued, but I was scared. *This way*, he said, *we get it over with.* I said I was sorry, and I rolled up my sleeping bag and left, walking home in the middle of the night, past the volunteer firehouse. A few volunteer firemen out front smoking cigarettes watched me go by. For months, I wondered what he meant by that. Get it over with.

Then there's this friend who goes to church. He really believes in god. This used to bother me, but as I've gotten older, I've become more forgiving. He asked me to be the godfather of his daughter. *It's okay that I don't believe?* I asked him. *Yes,* he said. *Totally fine*, he said. It's not going to be that thing where I have to stand up there in front of everyone and renounce Satan? I asked, thinking of the scene in *The Godfather. They don't do that sort of thing at my church,* he said. When I think about it now, it's funny to me that I was more concerned about maintaining my atheism than the possibility of raising my friend's daughter if he and his wife were killed in an accident. I agreed to do it and drove to West Virginia. I arrived the day before the ceremony and spent a really nice evening with my friend and his wife and her friend who was going to be the godmother. I got a little drunk and wondered what the status was for a godfather and a godmother, if we weren't a little bit married. The next morning, I put on a suit and tie and looked at myself in the mirror. *You're going to be someone's godfather,* I thought to myself. Your friends put you in positions where you never thought you'd be.

Like the time back in grad school when another friend of mine convinced me to drive out to the suburbs with two women from the Comp-Lit program and break into someone's backyard to swim in their pool. This friend had it on good authority, he said, that the family who owned the house was out of town. Who knows how he knew that? He is one of those people who have information. But I was the one with the car, so I was the hero. I got us there. It was one of those soupy St. Louis nights in early summer. On the warm concrete ringing the pool, we slipped out of our clothes. My friend's dashing smile flashed in the dark. I spent a half hour in the water talking to one of the Comp-Lit students about Lorrie Moore. Her breasts bobbed in front of her. I thought of my wife, back in the city on the couch with our dog, probably. I said I had to go home, sooner than my friend or the Comp-Lit students wanted to. My wife had recently miscarried, and I knew I ought to be sitting with her on the sofa, talking or not talking, instead of out in the suburbs, naked and trespassing.

In West Virginia, I leaned into the mirror and furrowed my brow to make it like Brando and mumbled like my mouth was full of cotton, *See how they massacred my boy.* My friend's church was one of those friendly, welcoming churches where the pastor seems like a normal person that could be your friend. She wore some kind of ceremonial garment, but it was casual as far as such items go. So I was surprised when, a few minutes into the ceremony, she asked my friend's wife's friend, the godmother, to repeat after her that she renounced Satan and his deeds. I tried to make eye contact with my friend, but his eyes stayed stuck to his daughter in her tiny white dress. And then the pastor looked right at me. Gone was the casual demeanor she'd maintained before, when we sipped coffee in the room behind the nave. Her eyes were stern, imploring. The baby, who had been asleep, began to babble. *Do you renounce Satan?* the pastor asked. *And all his works?* I had no choice but to say the words. *Yes,* I said. *I do renounce them.*

I remember being at a formal function, a wedding or bar mitzvah, when the DJ played Dionne Warwick's "That's What Friends Are For," and my mother and her friends and some of my aunts rushed to the dance floor even though it isn't really a rush-the-dance-floor kind of song. They put their arms around each other and just started singing along, swaying to the music. My mother had lost some weight, and I could tell she was proud to be up there, in the center of this group of women, the skinniest one. They raised their heads to the ceiling and sang the chorus. *Knowing you can always count on me, for sure.* It was embarrassing to see my mother singing, but I kept watching. Waving as a body, eyes closed, they seemed to have come together in this moment, over this song, in order to re-form a bond that was ancient and unknowable to me, something among women. Then the song was over, and they disentangled themselves from each other and left the dance floor to sit down next to their husbands.

I'm not one of your god-damn friends is something my father used to say when I was a kid. Now my father is losing his memory. Sometimes when I call, I can tell he doesn't quite know who I am. I think he thinks I might be one of his friends.

March 2021

Take the Bus Home

Suzy Eynon

I can always go back. I can never go back. I can go back, but I'll end up at a bowling alley watching my former roommate snort crushed pills in the parking lot. I'll go to the restroom, and when I return, I won't touch my beer, left to sweat on the table in my absence, just in case. I can't get back because I'm afraid of flying. I can get back, but I'll have to take the bus. *The Old Dog*, another passenger calls it. Boulder to Phoenix via Denver to Colorado Springs, Albuquerque, Grants, Gallup, Holbrook, Flagstaff. *This will be good for you,* my dad says, *to watch the land go by from the bus window as you pass over it.* I count the miles as the landscape shifts from evergreen to dust. I absorb how far I've gone from home and how far I have yet to go. Carry a map even though I'm not navigating. Measure the distance in pre-packaged gas station sandwiches until my stomach howls, until it hurts to shift my arms and legs, until I submit to the seat. I'm fine with never leaving the confines of this bus. Hug my backpack to my body as I sleep so no one steals it. I can arrive safely if I remain constantly, painfully aware. Accept food from neither of the men who offer it. Look away from the man who boards with the unbuttoned white shirt, his chest hair and heart surgery scar and smile all showing teeth. Look away from the dead worm wedged into the fabric of the seat I face for half the trip. Did it get stuck there to die, was it almost home? Most of the journey passes in the darkness of night and feels to primarily take place in New Mexico, even though that's not possible. Overnight, each person claims two seats or a row to themselves, seat-beds, legs flung over armrests, armrests jammed into spines as if our bodies can never fully unplug from the infrastructure of the rolling tube. Some play cards. The interior fills with pale mustard light. The world outside the windows is snuffed by a pitch-black blanket, the darkest dark. All I know is the inside of the bus. The bus careens down the road, a moment away from spinning out of control and over the side of a mountain road. The driver lets on single passengers at random spots in a tiny town, by stop signs, on the side of the freeway. He catches up with his new friends and laughs as if he is not singularly responsible for the lives and possible deaths of several sleeping passengers. I pass the dark hours clutching a plastic pig-shaped flashlight, a toy, its dim rays the sole beacon of optimism illuminating the pages of a book I don't care to read, my hand-held tie to reality, to the morning that will hopefully arrive. At dawn, I'm in Albuquerque. Halfway home. Too far along to turn back.

December 2022

FAMILY

The Miracle Jar

Thad DeVassie

Arriving at a time my father isn't home, I decide to clean out the refrigerator—not in the same way I did as a teenager with a voracious appetite, but as the adult child concerned for his aging parent, alone. I go about my business, tossing out salad dressings, things that appear overly pickled, and bags of store-bought shredded cheese nearly a decade old, barely showing the white, fleck-fuzz of decay. Half of the items resting at a comfortable thirty-seven degrees have to go.

When he arrives home after visiting mom at the memory care facility, I am scraping down his web-infested grill, prepping it for its first firing of the season in late August. I cook up hamburgers and few hot dogs he can have as leftovers. I bring the plate of steaming meat back inside where I see him rummaging through the refrigerator, mumbling to himself. I know what he is after—the four-year-old mayonnaise that I rinsed down the drain earlier. But he finds an acceptable alternative: a squat-sized container of Miracle Whip that I somehow overlooked.

He gasps, hit with the pungent smells of expiration, and I feel a hint of righteousness bubbling up inside of me in support of my afternoon's work. I begin prepping a short lecture in my mind about not letting food and condiments spoil and tossing them if they do.

But instead, he pulls a neatly folded rag out of the jar. I look on, perplexed. He explains how he painted the inside of the canister to make it look like the natural contents and to conceal the purple-colored Crown Royal sleeve that feels entirely too luxurious to be jammed into a refrigerated jar. When he unrolls the velvety rag, my mother's wedding ring and all of her precious pieces of jewelry are on display. For a moment, he plays the role of expert gemologist while I look on in disbelief at all that sparkles.

I hid these from your mother. She was hiding anything of value to her throughout the house; I didn't want to lose them. It made sense in a kind of twisted logic I would expect from my nine-year-old. He must have concocted this capsule a year or more ago, before her memory and antics became a toll too much for him to handle on his own.

It's his relief in finding them, believing they were lost forever, that I find so jarring. Here is a man who painted the inside of a container to the match the exact egg white and mustardy hue of Miracle Whip, yet couldn't remember doing so. How could someone be unable to extract from their mind the peculiarity of applying the perfect tint of paint to the oddest of canvases?

Then, in my own head, I hear a different kind of lecture: *Forget it.*

February 2021

Childhood

David Shields

What's your background?

Yes, just in general—what is your background?

Where did you grow up?

What were your parents like?

Are they still alive?

Do you have siblings?

Were you raised in a religious family?

Standard West Coast deracinated, detribalized Jewish secularism?

This is a photo of the rather humble house in which you grew up?

You may be weary of this line of questioning, but why do you keep writing about the same material over and over?

Is this art or repetition compulsion, if you know what I mean?

Essay or therapy?

If you're remembering something from fifty years ago, to what extent are you comfortable calling that "true"?

Now your father—he wrote for the New York Herald Tribune, right?

And your mother wrote for the *Nation*, right?

Were you as obsessed with the "Cyclops" TV column in the *Times* in the early 1970s as I was?

When did you realize that John Leonard was writing that column?

Didn't your cousin know him or something?

They worked together on the *Daily Cal* during the Free Speech Movement at Berkeley? Sounds so mythical.

Did Joan Baez really sing at your sixteenth birthday party?

You guys knew Tom Hayden and that crowd?

Mario Savio and his posse?

Alan Cranston—didn't your dad work for him briefly?

So, amidst Golden Gate Park anti-war demonstrations and flower power and R. Crumb and DROP ACID NOT BOMBS, where were you?

Who was little Davy Shields?

Card-carrying polemicist or incipient satirist?

Another way to say this is, your politics are a curious mix of lefty insurrection and rightist disdain—where are you in all this?

Are you William F. Buckley or William Lloyd Garrison?

Are you hanging out or a hanging judge—get my drift?

Do you share with me a profound antipathy toward everything Didion has become?

Was she an important influence you had to shed?

What influence if any were all the New Journalists you were assiduously reading in the then Bay Area-based *Rolling Stone*?

Hunter Thompson?

Joe Eszterhas?

Sara Davidson?

Et al.?

Paul Beatty says that everything that has made life even slightly livable in the 21st century was invented on the West Coast. Do you think this is true or do you just love anything that animates in you the East Coast/West Coast dialectic?

You like to say you peeked behind the domestic curtain to spy a very vulnerable and weak Wizard of Oz; what does that mean, in a political context?

How, for you, is it somehow connected to Kundera and his rabid anti-Communism?

What mind of kid were you?

"Mind"?

Did I say "mind"?

What *kind* of kid were you?

Jock?

Basket case?

Both of the above?

How did your parents process the fact that you were becoming a writer as well?

Did they live long enough to see you become the perpetual *enfant terrible* you've become?

Were they proud of you?

Competitive in what sense?

Are you competitive at all with your daughter (whose graphic memoir I've read and like at least as much as anything you've done of late)?

Is there a sense in which your work is *prima facie* evidence of untreated PTSD?

You've now written at least two—and one could easily say more like several—books about growing up, more or less; inevitable question: what gives?

You weren't raised in a gulag or Nazi Germany or by wolves. When are you going to grow up, some might ask?

Your father's name was Milton Schildkraut—that's for real?

That was his name until he changed it after the war?

Due to anti-Semitism or anti-German sentiment or both?

Do you see yourself as a German Jew?

A Jewish-American?

Your mom's "maiden name" was really Hannah Rochelle Schevill?

Is your personality—to the degree you think of yourself having a quite specific one—closer to your mother's or your father's?

Your so-called work ethic—where does that come from?

How about your "humor"—Mom or Dad?

Whence the angst?

Could you see ever being able to flip that feeling (or perhaps lack of feeling) into something truly positive and productive?

I seem to recall one reviewer saying you "articulate and exemplify the endemic disease of our time—the difficulty of feeling." *Touché?*

Ever think you'll feel anything again for real?

Would you call yourself a troublemaker as a tyke?

If you hadn't become a writer, what would you have done?

Would you have survived the regimen required?

Is the Philoctitean wound-and-the-bow your single deepest narrative vector or only your most insistent?

Do you think that each of us becomes, in the end, pure persona?

Does anyone ever get beyond his own mask?

Mask upon mask? I get it.

Where do you fall, by the way, on the paranoia meter vis-à-vis coronavirus? So far you don't seem to me insanely trepidatious.

Are you seeking an exit strategy?

How aggressively?

How self-destructively?

That incredible photo of you hitting the tape at the end of the 100-yard dash—where did all that light in your eyes go, Mr. Shields?

January 2021

Novels

D.T. Robbins

My brother sends me a text saying he and my sister-in-law are hurt and annoyed that my wife and I are pregnant at the same time as them. That it's weird and seems purposeful. That my wife did it intentionally just so she could be pregnant at the same time as my sister-in-law because she told them about a dream she had where this happened and then—*poof*—it happened! My wife, the witch, using her black magic to get knocked up as soon as she found out they were knocked up. She'd taken out a Ziplock bag with the blood of sacrificed children from the reserves in the garage freezer, ate a few scrambled snake eggs, went into a trance, and offered her soul to Satan in exchange for this small favor. He says our pregnancy will just overshadow theirs. He says they're actively taking a step back from us and that he doesn't owe me a conversation about it.

I text back, I disagree but thanks for telling me how you feel.

My wife is in the next room, bawling on the phone to her mom.

I call my mom. I don't know why I call my mom. We haven't talked much since she got pissed and lashed out and boycotted our post-Covid wedding reception because I invited my dad. I love my dad. My mom hates my dad. They've been divorced for over twenty years. The fairytales got it wrong. Sometimes hate is stronger than love. I tell my mom about the text my brother just sent me. She acts surprised. She says she had no idea about any of this. She says she gets where he's coming from.

I write a novel in my notes app. It's a collection of the same letter to my brother written and rewritten in various iterations.

Some of the letters go like this: This situation feels really unfair.

Some of the letters go like this: Fuck you, you entitled asshole!

My novel reaches 50,000,000 words. It's the longest novel ever written. Longer than the Bible. It wraps around the planet twice. I recite the novel in my car on the way to work. I practice it daily. In my head and out loud. In the mirror. In the night sky. Directly into the sun. I methodically pick apart the novel to figure out which words and sentences and arguments I want to emphasize. Which to raise my voice on and which to whisper. I rehearse it over and over. It's both my best and my worst work. I delete the novel entirely. I tell myself to let it go. I tell myself to forgive him. I tell myself to let karma do its thing. I rewrite the novel. This time it's over 1,000,000,000 words and in every known human language in the history of known human languages. I write until my fingertips start to bleed and my flesh falls off and the bones stick out. I write it in blood.

My wife doesn't like to talk about it. Talking about it makes her cry. Thinking about it makes her cry. But when she does talk about it, she says, "I just feel so stupid."

I say, "You're not stupid."

She says, "People get pregnant at the same time all the fucking time."

I say, "I know. I don't get it."

I tell my mom we won't be doing the family Christmas this year. My mom says fine, but she wants to spend some time with my two older kids. I say ok, but please don't bring them around my brother and sister-in-law because of the situation. My mom tells me I'm putting her in the middle. That I'm punishing her by giving her this stipulation. That she wasn't planning on bringing the kids around them, but nevermind now, she just won't spend any time with the kids at all. She writes it in all caps LIKE THIS.

I say ok, have a good holiday.

My oldest daughter starts asking why we haven't seen her uncle and aunt in a long time. I tell her that sometimes grown-ups need a break from each other. She asks if they know she's going to be a big sister again. I tell her they do and that they're going to have a baby too, so she'll also have a little cousin. She gets real excited and tells her brother, and he gets real excited. They're both excited and my wife tries not to cry, and I try to smile, and we both pretend nothing is broken.

I talk to my brother in my head. I argue with my brother in my head. I scream at my brother in my head. I break his fucking jaw in my head. I help him up and ask if he's ok. He says he's sorry and he was being a dumbass, and we're brothers again. Then something reminds me of his text, and I start the whole fucking thing over in my head.

I tell my wife, "I'm sorry I talk about my brother so much."

She says, "Don't be sorry. It's your family, and I know it hurts you more than it hurts me. I don't know what I'd do if my brother had reacted this way."

My wife and her mom plan the baby shower. My oldest daughter asks if we're going to invite her uncle and aunt. I say probably not. She asks if they're going to have a baby shower and if she'll be invited. I want to lie to her and tell her of course, they love you, why wouldn't they invite you? But I tell her the truth. I tell her they already had their baby shower, and we weren't invited. She cries for a really long time in my arms, and I tell my brother you did this, you motherfucker, in my head over and over and over, and I hope he hears me and it melts his brain.

My mom says she's tentatively planning on going to the baby shower. She doesn't go. She gives no explanation why. She went to their baby shower. Then they have another baby shower that's just with their friends, and she goes to that one too.

I start a new novel that goes like this: Fuck you, mom! Fuck you! Fuck you! Fuck you!

My brother sends me a text with a picture of his son telling me I'm an uncle and he loves me, and he hopes we can talk and work things out. I tell him congratulations and that his son is beautiful. I don't say anything else. I don't tell him how shitty it is to expect me to celebrate the birth of his baby when he's already cast a dark cloud over mine before she's even born.

I go insane. I work out every day. I dissociate. I drink too much. I hate myself for not standing up for myself. I think I'm a coward. I think I'm a coward who lets anyone and everyone walk all over him, and that's all I'll ever be. I think my wife should have married a real man who will fight for her. I think my kids deserve a better, stronger father. I meditate. I go on walks. I read self-help books and watch YouTube videos about family trauma and imagine a world where I'm an orphan and what a wonderful world it is to live in.

At thirty-six weeks, the doctor says our baby isn't growing. She says my wife needs to be induced ASAP. My wife is in labor for over thirty hours before the nurse tells us the umbilical cord is wrapped around our baby's neck and they need to cut my wife open ASAP. My wife shakes and cries. She signs the paperwork saying if she dies it's not the hospital's fault. She calls her mom and her mom tells her it's going to be ok. The nurses make me wait for a million years before letting me into the operating room where my wife is stretched out like Jesus Christ on his cross. The doctors are cutting and pulling, and my wife is crying, and I'm telling her everything is going to be ok. I tell her I'm here and everything will be ok even though I can't do shit if something does go wrong. From my wife's flesh, the doctors pull out our baby girl. She cries, and it's the most beautiful sound we've ever heard. The sun pulls the roof off from above us and shines down on her and tears cover our faces, and I tell my wife, you did it! She's here! We spend three more days in the hospital nursing our baby and changing our baby and introducing our baby to everyone and everything and saying this was all made for you. I don't send my brother a text with a picture of my baby.

I decide I need therapy. I read my brother's text to my therapist. I read my mom's text to my therapist. I tell her all about my life, all about my family. She says she can't diagnose it, but it sounds like my mom might have borderline personality disorder. I tell her that my brother's therapist told him the same thing. She says it sounds like my brother is going through a lot, and it doesn't really have to do with me, but because of the family dynamic my mom created, I'm the one who takes the brunt of it. She tells me I was a parentified child to an emotionally immature parent. She asks, have I ever heard of emotional incest? She tells me issues like this are common among siblings of parents with BPD. She says it sounds like I'm the scapegoat of my family dynamic and my brother is likely often the golden child. I feel less crazy. I feel like my brain isn't a runny mess of goo anymore. I feel alive. I can see the skyline and the stars, and I can feel the wind on my face and all five senses are working again. She asks why I never took my brother up on talking or working things out. I tell her I'm not sure. She calls bullshit. I tell her the truth, and the truth is that I'm scared I'll either lose my shit or let him walk all over me again. She says that's fine, but I should at least try. I say fine. We spend the next couple months writing a new novel. I write a draft and read it to my therapist. She tells me I need to revise this and not say that or be more direct and be less aggressive. It goes through ten thousand rounds of edits. I practice this novel out loud and in my head every day. I read it to my therapist who pretends to be my brother and starts to look like my brother and talk like my brother.

We whittle the novel down to a short email that goes like this: I'm sorry you've felt overshadowed. That's a shitty feeling, but it didn't warrant your reaction. I know you wanted this life event to yourself but life doesn't work that way. What you said felt intentionally hurtful, and I can't allow that kind of behavior around my family. We're not responsible for your insecurities or jealousies, and we shouldn't be treated as though we are. I love you. Good luck. Take care.

I click send and the email goes through the sky past the birds and the planes and the memories of better times and so long, goodbye.

For the next few weeks, the only sound I hear is static. My brother never responds. I text him to ask if he got my email. No response there either.

The world slowly opens, and I hear my baby's laugh. I watch my two older kids get excited when they play with her. I watch my wife grow into motherhood. I watch my in-laws fall in love with their first grandbaby. I watch my baby's hair grow blonde and curly and her eyes turn blue and her smile grow big and her teeth come in. I watch her turn one and learn to walk. I hear her call her brother bro bro and her sister sissy even though she says it with a lisp and it sounds like thi-thee. I watch my older kids play soccer and perform in plays and get braces. My wife dyes her hair from red to blonde, and after I beg her, she dyes it back to red because red is sexy as fuck on her. We redo our backyard. We buy my wife a new mom car. We go to New Orleans with some friends, and I see family on my mom's side who love me, and they ask about our baby and bring us gifts for our baby and tell me how beautiful all my kids are. I publish a book, and my friends buy it and come to my readings and tell me good job. I talk about future plans with my wife. Like wanting to open a bookstore someday in a small town. I decide to start publishing books by other writers. I start a new novel. It goes like this: It's whatever I want it to be and has nothing to do with my family. The past and the pain shrink behind me. It doesn't leave, but it doesn't matter. They're still there. In my notes app. In my emails. In my text messages. Life grows around them in full bloom until I don't see them. Until I don't feel them. Until life is bigger than they ever were.

July 2023

In Which I Tell Strangers My Uncle Is Satan

Kirsti MacKenzie

When the time is right, I go: *You wanna hear something fuckin' crazy?*

This is five-or-six-drinks-in kind of shit. For rooms that smell like stale beer and coke sweats. For strangers on barstools. For girls ugly-crying in the bathroom. For nerds in corners. There's an art to it, and you can't go fucking it up. Not after starting like that.

I go: *My uncle is Satan.*

This isn't my story, but I tell it anyway. Nothing too crazy about me. Grew up nice and safe in a little subdivision. Summers on the lake. Straight A's. Spring breaks in Florida. Two parents that stayed together. Two college degrees. Two dick boyfriends til I had a nice one. What do I really have to say about myself at a party?

I go: *Uncle Satan wasn't always Satan. Satan used to be Brian, and Brian's a political shit disturber. There were clown suits and Godzilla costumes involved. Have you heard of the Rhino party? Google that shit. Yes, like the zoo animal. They platformed repealing the law of gravity and putting the national debt on VISA. Wild shit. Anyway—Brian became head Rhino.*

I tell this story to strangers because I couldn't tell it to Dad. Shame because Dad has a real good sense of humor. Loves absurd shit. Instead of writing term papers or whatever I was supposed to be doing for my fancy little degree, I googled Brian instead, and there he was: crazy Uncle Satan. With my laptop humming and hot on my forearm, I followed Dad around the kitchen, and he said *Jesus Christ, enough. I don't wanna hear it.*

I go: *Anyway, Brian and the Rhinos wanna be big shots, so he sues the fed for party status. Now, here's where it gets fuckin' crazy. Brian falls in love, right? She said she'd only marry the devil himself, so Brian changes his name. Satan, or Sa Tan, haha. She turns him down. He sues the fed for fifty mil, and because this country's a constitutional monarchy, because this son of a bitch fell in love, the lawsuit gets filed as—get this—Satan versus Her Majesty the Queen.*

Dad doesn't wanna hear it because he's lived the shit that compels a person to become the prince of darkness on paper. Fathers that drank too much and mothers in psych wards and other brothers, ones that died before they hit thirty. Foster homes and fractured lives. Things I know nothing about, because it's a minor fucking miracle he chose to be steady—not Satan. I tell this story because the real one is too sad.

I go: *Here's the kicker. Last week my aunt emails me out of the blue. Tells me we're direct descendants of Christ himself because we have red hair, and she fires a YouTube link in there to prove it. Who the fuck am I to argue with a YouTube link? So now you can leave this bar and say: today I met the devil and god. Next round's on you.*

April 2023

SANDY POINT
Andrew Sottile

There's an island called Sandy Point where Long Island Sound pours into the Atlantic.

Nona and Pa lived on the mainland in Mystic. Once, Nona remarked to the dinner table that we were an especially strange family. This was Thanksgiving or Easter. Maybe someone's birthday. Nona was kidding, of course. I couldn't have been seven.

I blurted out, Especially Ruthie.

Nona took me to the little back room and told me to apologize for what I said. So I did.

Auntie Ruth's been through a lot, Nona said. She had operations. Kids picked on her about her scars. Bullies is what they are. She had a hard time with the drink, Nona said. That's why Ruthie kept dogs—they wouldn't judge. Nona and Pa bought her a Subaru, and while Ruthie was inside at a twelve-step meeting, the dogs tore the car's upholstery down to foam.

When I was still a baby, my mother uneasily agreed to let newly sober Ruthie watch after me. That night, Ruthie called my mother and father's restaurant and said she'd gotten into the Rolling Rock ponies in the fridge. She was sorry but someone needed to come home.

Eventually Ruthie got sober for good. She married a man named Lanny who sold Fords in New London. Lanny kept a boat outside and stayed up late tinkering with the engine, smoking cigarettes on the cement steps beneath the carport.

Nona and Pa picked me up from school most Fridays, and I'd spend the night with them. One day, Ruthie called for me on the phone. She wondered would I come stay with her and Lanny. Only if I wanted. She'd understand if not.

Sometime later, Lanny's boat was seaworthy, and I spent Friday night with him and Ruthie. Saturday morning we trailered to Noank and launched into the Mystic River. It was hot and calm, but on the Sound there were swells. We spotted a flopping sunfish the size of a dinner table. Lanny let me take the helm. Ruthie sat with the dogs. It seemed strange to steer from the right side of the boat. I wouldn't have known to say *starboard.* There were no pedals I couldn't reach, and the speed was controlled by hand. We skipped over waves, and all seemed fine until we were deep in a trough and Lanny strong-armed the wheel away from me. He deemed I'd put us in danger and told me as much. Maybe I had.

Before long we anchored and swam off Sandy Point. It's where Rhode Island meets Connecticut meets New York. In the shallows stands the remains of an eighteenth-century warehouse where a man called Rhodes hid his liquor. Rhodes' Folly, locals called it. Lore has it that to avoid paying tax, he moved his supply around, from state to state but under the same roof, so inspectors couldn't confirm in whose jurisdiction his stash was stored.

That day on the water, no one mentioned Rhodes or his liquor scheme. The dogs were fetching off the bow of the boat in long bounds and splashes. I asked Lanny and Ruthie about the stone pyramid rising from the clear blue shallows, and someone thought it would be fun to go climb it. It might have been me. Likely it was me.

What happened next happened fast. I leapt from the stern and swam to shore. Lanny and Ruthie and the dogs did too. Then I was climbing the great remains of Rhodes' warehouse. Hands and feet on the granite. The dogs were climbing too. A paw nicked me. Then I fell. I remember the sound more than the pain. The hollow splash of water, stone, and bone. I tried to stand and gimped off into the sand.

Immediately I understood I was to hide this from everyone. Nothing seemed broken, I said. Ruthie agreed I wouldn't mention it to Nona and Pa, that I wouldn't share what happened with my parents. No damage done.

My father, Ruthie's little brother, met us back at the boat trailer. I launched into a lie about how earlier in the week I'd kicked the mission oak chair in the basement playing soccer, and hadn't he and my mother noticed my limp? I suppose I used my secret with Ruthie to make my father feel neglectful. That's a thing I did. Something about a day on the water had aggravated it, I said. He never asked about it again.

I told my mother the lie, told Nona and Pa the lie. I even told everyone at school the lie. No fun story about how I fell from several feet up while out at sea.

Thirty years beyond it, and no one knows the colossal disaster Ruthie avoided. It's true I think of it that way. It's not that I avoided disaster—though surely I did—it's that Ruthie did. All that could have shaken the family's unflinching love for her was if something happened to me, the only grandkid, while she was looking after me. The boy who fell into the sandy shallows, not onto the rocks, and then kept his mouth shut about it. It was an accident. But it wasn't. It wasn't something that happened and Ruthie happened to be on watch. It was her and her husband and their dogs and their boat and their blessing that willed my fall into the world.

I have a son now. It's astounding to think I was allowed to go on Lanny's boat. But my parents were overworked, glad for time alone, for childcare on a Friday night. Of course I was safe with family. It's possible Ruthie and Lanny, and even Nona and Pa, just mentioned in passing a low-speed cruise up the river, that they spoke in half-truths and fudged the plan to motor east-by-southeast toward the north Atlantic.

That Nona and Pa thought it was good for me to spend time with Ruthie is less surprising. They wanted their daughter, their first born, the one who'd been teased, to care for and love and be loved by their grandson. At least she could be an auntie, they said. That was something. They imagined Ruthie and me on beaches, cruising in Lanny's boat on calm, balmy days.

I feel it now on cool mornings. I wish I could call it Ruthie's ankle, but there's been other missteps since. A skipped stair, a mossy root.

January 2021

Seizures

Amy Lyons

Age 8

Your mother has a seizure on the front lawn after grocery shopping, and you stand there wondering what you'll have for dinner as a can of peas and a jar of sauce roll into the cul-de-sac where you ride your bike and play freeze tag. An ambulance swallows her. Eleven months later, you'll watch her gleaming coffin lowered into the dull dirt, and you'll watch your father slowly spiral into relentless grief that lays waste to your house until the bank finally forecloses, and you move from apartment to apartment to apartment.

Age 12

You writhe on the bed and bleed through the maxi pad, your underwear, your shorts, the sheets, the mattress. Is this what happened to your mother on the lawn? Is the ambulance coming for you like a shark who smells your blood? While you sweat and shake, Billy Idol sneers from one of countless rock posters wallpapering your bedroom: *hey little sister, what have you done?* Your father says you have to go the emergency room because it wasn't like this when your sisters got theirs. You agree to go to the hospital but please, you say—pain burrowing into your back and blazing through your belly—not in an ambulance. The day your body gains the ability to have babies will always live in your mind as a medical emergency, but the doctor says there's nothing wrong and hands your father a slip of paper for the pharmacy. The next day you start fifth grade dressed in your plaid Catholic jumper, a super-winged maxi pad, double underwear, shorts, tights, and a backpack slung over your shoulder with a bottle of prescription painkillers rattling inside it. The nuns will never know.

Age thirty years before birth

Your father is a monk, and for reasons he'll never reveal, he leaves the seminary before they make him a Catholic priest. He meets your mother, marries, has three daughters. He'll share with you fragments about his holy life, and the one detail that sticks is the way his mother felt when he stopped short of priesthood: deeply disappointed. You'll meet your grandmother a half-dozen times, and you'll always see that nun-like look of disappointment when she lays her eyes upon her son.

Age 48

The pregnant women you study at your job take anti-epileptic drugs (AEDs) and you track the rate of AED-associated malformations in their babies: clubbed foot, a hole in the abdominal wall out of which the baby's intestines spill, cleft lip, an extra digit. In some cases, the babies won't make it and the mothers will wonder what they did wrong. Call scripts keep the conversations clinical. You ask questions about their menstrual cycles, the nature and cause of their seizures, the time that elapses between their awareness of an approaching seizure and the seizure itself.

Age 8

Five minutes before your mother's seizure, she's driving, and you're in the back seat, pouting because she didn't get you an Almond Joy at the grocery store. She doesn't shake and slump and lose control of the vehicle. Her eyes don't roll back, and she doesn't careen you off the road into oncoming traffic or flip the Toyota into that ditch near the woods where the big kids smoke Marlboro reds. You don't die dangling upside down, trapped inside your safety belt while the engine explodes. Your car doesn't submerge itself in the Charles. You don't drown.

Age 48

There's a question in the call script about fertility history.

Age 37

You've peed on pink sticks over many months, and the minus signs make you wonder what the prescription painkillers you started taking with that first period have masked all these decades. "Endometriosis," your dead mother might have said, "let's get you some help." You should have started trying to conceive sooner, but in therapy, you couldn't work through mothering without a mother, and you couldn't figure out who would take care of your father—who isn't yet sick but is as penniless as the priest he didn't become—if you're an overwhelmed mother. You, as it will turn out, four years from now, that's who. Your sisters won't have the bandwidth; they're motherless mothers.

Age 48
There's a question in the call script about past pregnancy outcomes.

Age 38
Your period is late, and you've agreed not to obsess over minus signs so instead, you and your husband go on vacation and rip through a rippling rink of deep sea. You crank the jet ski's handle harder, faster, and you're free, and you're scared, and you're laughing, and you're madly in love, and you're high on the press of his chest on your back, hungry for more salty spray on your tongue, elated by the speed and buck of the machine between your legs. That night, you bleed through your underwear, your shorts, the bedsheets. What slides thick and sinewy out of your body in the flipped condo bathroom with the faux-marble vanity looks like a massacre. You'll wonder forever if a baby would have arrived nine months later had you remained vigilant with those sticks, stayed still and silent as a cloistered monk, prayed, kept faith.

Age 39
After moving in and out of two dozen apartments, you buy a townhouse because you can't afford a house that looks like the one where your mother seized before the bank seized it, but you want to own your home so you won't end up in a two-room, low-income apartment in Revere like your faithful widower father, who has just enough space for his TV, his armchair, his beat-up bed, a second-hand table stacked with unfinished crossword puzzles and yellowing funeral prayer cards.

Age 8-48
At the after-party for your mother's funeral, an aunt says your mother is in a better place, and for the next three-plus decades you move from apartment to apartment from state to state from job to job from relationship to relationship from teacher to teacher to teacher to psychiatrist to guru to nutritionist to diet quack to book coach to priest to healer to massage therapist to professor to fertility doctor looking for that place.

Age 42
Your father has a seizure when you're transferring him from the bed to the wheelchair in the living room of the townhouse you thank God you bought because where else would your father live in his final months? Not in the nursing home where he lived for two weeks before you sprung him, where you visited him and asked what you could bring him, and he said a loaded gun. Here, in your townhouse, the seizure is a classic grand mal, and he's shaking and drooling, and his eyes are rolling to the whites, and you can't just stand there like a helpless eight-year-old while a neighbor presses a spoon to your mother's tongue and your sister runs to the end of the street to flag the ambulance. You're the adult, the caretaker here, so fucking *do* something. Move. You take your father to the doctor in a cab made for wheelchairs because distrust of ambulances runs in your family. The doctor says to call hospice. They show you how to drip morphine and Ativan into the soft pink flesh of your father's inner cheek from two vials with eye-droppers that you somehow manage not to lick, though you can taste the relief it would bring, like when you were eight on that one blazing summer afternoon, and you looked at the sky and opened your mouth to swallow sudden rain.

Age 48
Your moods swing like this essay's timeline when your husband gets a job and you move from a life you like in New York (you're renting again because your father died on morphine and Ativan you administered in that townhouse and his ghost won't move out) to a life you have no idea

how to lead in Tennessee. The psychiatrist's answer for short-term relief is Ativan. You fall asleep high, happy that you gave your father this relief as he slid toward heaven. Twelve hours later, you wake in a fog that lifts to unveil rage's sharp, whirling weather. You don't want to live here. You want to move. You want to live in that house on the cul-de-sac that you stake out every time you visit Boston.

Age 48
There's a question in the call script about reasons for taking an AED. Possible answers include epilepsy, pain, and mood disorder.

Age 48
The psychiatrist's long-term solution for your swinging moods is an AED, which you take for twelve days. The medication causes a whole new set of swings—from jitters to insomnia and back again. You stop because it's not like you're suffering from seizures or something. It's not like your moods really interfere with anything. You're not flailing on the front lawn. You're not moaning or choking or in any danger of hitting your head. You're not feeling the effects of a hidden brain tumor or trying to raise three daughters while also keeping your house clean and your marriage intact. You're just unable to function all that well a few days every month, around the time your period would come before it stopped coming when you were only forty-four. It's not like you're dying. It's just your spirit dimming and dimming and dimming.

Age 42
Your father is dying, but some part of your grief-stricken mind thinks you can save him. You and your husband wake up several times a night to put cold towels on his forehead and to transfer his weak body from the bed to the commode. You bathe him together, you hoist him from the floor like a pair of paramedics when he falls. Your husband shaves your father's sunken face over the kitchen sink. You make him oatmeal and raise cans of Ensure to his grey lips. You love taking care of him. Motherhood, you're made for it. You and your father play a child's card

game four weeks before he dies because your usual game of poker is too much for his foggy mind. You ask if he has a seven and wonder out loud who will take care of you like this when you're old and sick and shit out of luck. "You have to adopt a kid," he says, "go fish."

Age 43

The woman at the adoption agency says you and your husband seem perfect. You fill out a form. You back away from the process because you're desperate to make your body make a baby. The fertility doctor says your husband's sperm is stellar and your uterus looks amazing and a donor egg with IVF will give you excellent odds. You swing between yes and no, then step away from the process because you're sure it's grief and not a real desire to have a child that drives you. Your need to become a mother will strike for a few days at a time without warning for the next several years, like seizures that threaten to drive your mind off the road of your real life, your writing life, which you've only now managed to commit to fully after years of fits and starts.

Age 48

You're closing on a three-bedroom house in three weeks. You'll have a decent-sized office for the first time in your life. You'll have an empty bedroom that you won't rush to fill. Instead of quitting your job like you've done roughly every three years your whole life, you'll keep studying the pregnant women and their AED usage and the outcomes on their babies. You won't quit writing for months on end then try to remember where you left off. You won't move again, though you never expected to settle here. You'll stay. You'll have faith. You'll remain.

Age ____

You hear something you've heard a million times, but this time it sticks: Pattern stories come alive not when you make the pattern, but when you break it.

October 2022

My Brother Visits

Andrew Bertaina

Three months before my wife and I officially separate and I move into a one bedroom, my brother visits. He's a tenured college professor from Illinois, and though we're close, I don't talk much about the marriage. We aren't those kinds of brothers who share everything. He has an interest in ancient eastern culture, so we go to the museum that's housing the stele tablets with the Code of Hammurabi etched into them.

My brother peers around at the tablets, making meaning of the words, laws, promises and punishments that bind civilization together. He peers at the glass, whispers the Akkadian words to himself. I can't read a damn thing. The truth is, I'm mulling over the end of some things, the beginning of others. The past doesn't interest me much these days. I'm simple and more interested in the way the glass captures part of my face, an afterimage on the tablet, a suggestion of a second self.

The codes, a series of commercial regulations and judicial punishments, were written somewhere between 1792 and 1750 BC after Hammurabi united the series of cities scattered as seeds around the meeting point of the Tigres and the Euphrates.

I'd read recently that the primary reason human beings had moved from hunting and gathering to an agrarian society is because wheat is measurable, and therefore taxable. The move to settlements was the cause of massive disease spread and the beginning of a caste system we still see today. No more were people wandering through fields of water, frozen over by frost, feet cracking, as they listened for the distant rumble of the herd.

Years earlier, on my long and almost unending career detour, I taught eighth-graders about the lush river lands around the Tigres and the Euphrates. I was working as a classroom assistant then in a school where the kids routinely ran out of the classroom and mumbled fuck you under their breath.

I spent those months at the school, flailing away, while my marriage lost the last of its shape, buried under an avalanche of diapers and appointments and disconnection. My mentor at the job was concerned with my lessons. She was worried I wasn't learning enough about how to teach eighth graders. I was learning that I had no desire to teach people who didn't give a fuck. And maybe my wife was learning the same thing about me as she was with our two and four year-olds, and I spent my available hours with co-workers, drinking or dancing, letting the thing go.

I wish I had the same ability to bring order to the world like my brother, he of five languages, and the stable marriage. He owns his own house, has a Fulbright, and is fully vested in his 401K. And there he sits, decoding the laws, the penalties for breaking promises.

I stand watching him, my mind in a state of constant disorder, not fully vested in my 403B, confused as to the muck I'd dragged my life into. At best, they'd pull me up like those mammoths from the tar pits, marveling at the way I'd managed to be preserved by the tar, by the stele.

Weeks after my brother departs, my wife of thirteen years and I officially split after a year of agonizing indecision, nights on the couch downstairs, texting other people in the hollow cavern of cell phone light. I move a few essential items into my new apartment, into my new life—T-shirts, blue jeans, a futon. In the nearly empty living room, I imagine a different life, the only damn thing my imagination has ever been useful for, walls full of photography from future trips to Europe—sun-washed courtyards, cathedrals piercing skies, vineyards on the hilltops above the city and distant denim skies. This apartment, I think, will always be full of wine and friends and laughter.

But life isn't etched into stele. In the morning, I awoke alone, knowing I needed to find a bunk bed before next weekend.

June 2021

HEARTBREAK

Silicification

Brianna Snow

I.

My name rhymes with yours, so I cut off two syllables. We're no twinning lesbian couple. I can't look directly at you. Yes, you're short. But that's not it.

I love you day to day, Leana. I widen the gap in me for you. You want to be a mother. I kiss your stomach, like the forehead of a child.

I listen to all the sad gay songs on city walks. Everyone is going to a funeral or dreading December or tying a belt around their neck. You promise to teach me the drums. I hold you while your phone plays "In Your Eyes." You tap the beat on my thigh and try to see if your nose fits in my ear.

You roll a pair of your socks onto my cold feet. And bring the blanket from the couch.

II.

The government sends you to a desert on the West Coast, then one in the Middle East. Whatever undisclosed things they have you do put scotch and sleeping pills on the nightstand.

I pack light. Dildos must remain in the closet. You brief the embassy about who I am to you. Nothing suspicious makes it through customs, and here I am with no cover.

You drive me to the Red Sea. You know I want to swim in all the water in the world. You plan more trips, braid my hair in hotels. We float on the Dead Sea.

I buy us cake to eat in bed. You remove all our clothes to feed me crumbs because we can only hug at the airport. I taste pistachio the whole trip back to the empty couch in DC.

You get drunk with a married woman who wants to fuck you. You cry and cry on the phone, and I can't hold you. You change your mind about me.

Between the balcony's rotted plants, I watch a black SUV drop you off. You smell different, like the hidden side of tinted windows. You kiss me and don't notice I don't want it.

III.

In the Valley of Fire sat a petrified log. Beside it, a plaque:

Millions of years ago, this tree likely grew with others of its kind in a forest several miles from here. Later, flood waters carried the fallen log to this area where it was buried beneath thousands of feet of silt, sand, and sea deposits. Here it slowly changed.

The log looked like a log behind a fence. No one had polished it to reveal opalized anything. There were folds of silence. There were no pickup trucks or camels or women.

If we stuck around any longer, you'd have turned to stone. And I wouldn't have left.

April 2023

IMAGINARY

Kaycie Hall

I found the letters tucked into an old journal. They fell out along with a sheet of old Photomaton pictures I'd used for my French ID. My eyes are wide, lips unsmiling and painted red, bangs cut crookedly because I used to do it myself with kitchen scissors. Of course I hadn't forgotten your letters, but I hadn't read them in a long time. They're folded tightly, one of them on the slick paper that you ripped out of our college graduation program; the page is indented under your words because you had to bear down so hard with the pen while writing to me through the commencement speech. The other is on notebook paper, written in pencil, faded from time. We were twenty-one, and you wrote "I think you're perfect and I'd do or change anything about myself in hopes of consistently making you smile." Your handwriting is cramped and scratchy.

I had a boyfriend then. I'd been with him all through college, and being in the deep South, it was expected that we'd get married soon because that's what people do. I didn't love him, but I'd never told you that. Whenever he tried to kiss me, I felt suffocated. I'd push him away and say it must be something in the air, allergies, the medication I'd taken that morning, maybe I was just tired.

I never told you that though. Instead, I sat down on the floor in my nearly empty dorm room and cried. Then I called you and said I'd love it if we could remain friends.

*

Your attentions went to my head. I loved my reflection in your eyes. I felt like a deity at whose feet you worshipped, even though I laughed away your admiration in conversations with my friends. Still, I liked you from afar. Once, you were in town and dropped by the bookstore where I worked as a surprise, but I hid from you in my car out back. I don't know if I was afraid of you or myself. I told my friends that you were stalking me, but actually I was flattered.

I read all of the books you recommended. I read *The Garden of Eden* by Hemingway even though I hate Hemingway. I loved it, but I'm still not sure if that's because I actually enjoyed it or because it reminded me of you.

Once when I was house-sitting, I thought about calling and asking you to come stay with me. I still had a boyfriend, but I wanted you, or I wanted the me that I was with you. I did call, but I didn't ask you to come over. Instead, we talked late into the night. You were sitting outside by your sister's pool, smoking cigarettes—I could hear you inhale and exhale. I knew you rolled them yourself. I'd watch you do it whenever we'd wait outside of the liberal arts building in college. I was curled up in a strange bed, my stomach aflutter from a mix of guilt and elation.

*

The year I worked in a bookstore, I sometimes flirted with the writers who came to do book signings. One attractive male author once strongly recommended that I read *A Sport and a Pastime,* a flirtation that I didn't understand until I actually read it a year later. I always bragged to you about these encounters. You were a writer too, and I wanted to make you jealous.

"I aspire to have someone write about me. I'd love to be a muse," I texted you.

"Really? That's pretty self-absorbed," you replied.

It stung—because you were right and I was fishing for you to say that I already was yours.

*

We didn't see each other for years. You dated other people. I stayed with the same guy. I'd see the photos of other women with you on Facebook, and I hated them. I loved it when you broke up with them and talked about how annoying they were, though you did feel bad about the girl in Yellowstone whose virginity you took. The petty part of me was pleased that I still won out in the battle for your affections, a virgin sacrifice to the altar of me.

*

In 2012, I came back from France after years of near constant communication, after finally saying "I love you" over the phone. I changed my flight to come home to you. I was nervous to see you in person, even though I'd been talking to you over Skype for the past year.

We were on opposite schedules then, life and time zone. I woke up early in the morning for class at the Sorbonne and would call you on Skype as you'd be returning from your late night restaurant shift in New Orleans. Throughout the call, I'd look at the small image of myself in the corner of the screen, applying my makeup, fascinated to see what my own features looked like as I did mundane things. You also looked at me. "You're so beautiful," you'd say, eyes half closing from exhaustion.

I had a layover in Dallas, where I changed clothes and put on makeup, hoping to look nice instead of exhausted after packing up my entire life and lugging it back to the States via eight-hour flight. When I landed in New Orleans, I played it cool, like always, afraid to show that anything or anyone mattered to me, especially you, who mattered so much. Your hands were shaking, and you were sweating nervously. When I hugged you, I felt the warm dampness of the back of your T-shirt.

*

On the page of my journal that I tucked your letters into, I wrote a quote from *Anna Karenina*. The entry is dated July 22, 2012, about three months after I'd come back to Louisiana. I must have been rereading Anna's story to find some solace in my own unhappiness at being back in the South, bored, and unexpectedly lonely.

What I had copied down was from a chapter where Vronsky is hours late to meet Anna:

> *She placed both hands on his shoulders and gazed at him for a long time with a deep, rapturous, and at the same time, searching look. She studied his face to make up for the time in which she had not seen him.*
>
> *As at every meeting, she was bringing together her imaginary idea of him (an incomparably better one, impossible in reality) with him as he was.*

You were different. I wondered if I'd somehow created an imaginary idea of you, of us. You were so angry, sometimes at me, sometimes at the world, but you directed it at me because I was there.

You'd moved into an apartment on Iberville Street in New Orleans, and I'd stay weekends with you, expecting us to make up for lost time, but you left me alone for long periods where I laid around on your bed, reading. Once you locked me in the apartment from the outside, saying I shouldn't leave, and then came back to grab some notebooks from on top of your fridge and angrily said "just in case you thought you could snoop while you're here."

Out of spite, I opened your laptop and read every document you had saved. None of it was worth anything. Useless fragments of term papers, starts of poems, garbage.

*

My close friends had planned a night out for my birthday. You arrived late, pissed off, aggressively possessive of me, forcing me to sit on your lap, too affectionate in front of everyone. I was uncomfortable.

You left early. I went home with my best friend, explaining that you were just stressed out, trying to wrap up your thesis while working nights. I didn't want her to see how sad I was, how disappointed, and after all, you were planning to make it up to me tomorrow; you'd gotten a room at a nice hotel downtown.

When we met up the next day, the air between us felt heavy. I was afraid, though I wasn't sure why. I didn't say anything as I got into the passenger seat of your car and you loaded my suitcase into the back.

"I need to stop by Spencer's," you said. "I left some medication that I need there."

"We haven't seen Spencer in a while," I said.

"He's not home. I'm just going in to pick something up."

I went inside with you and sat down on the couch while you went into the back. I didn't question why you brought, let alone left, medication to a friend's house. You came back into the living room, livid, yelling about how Spencer, your best friend, had stolen your medication.

"Why would he steal medicine from you?" I asked.

You picked up a pile of books on the coffee table and threw them across the room, so angry that you were close to tears. "Because he's a fucking asshole," you screamed.

I stood there, shocked and repulsed. I didn't mean to, but I started laughing. "You are acting like an idiot right now, and it's seriously unattractive," I said, walking outside to sit on the porch, willing my heartbeat to slow down.

I didn't know you were doing heroin regularly.

*

We imploded spectacularly. I kept searching for what I thought must have been the real you—I couldn't understand where the person I'd known and loved had gone. I started to feel crazy, like I'd completely imagined you, or like I could no longer trust my own judgements and feelings. The version of myself I'd fallen for, that lovely reflection in your eyes, withered and died. I'd become a burden to you. You told me, "Don't take this the wrong way, but I have a real life, and things that are bigger than you." I'd lost myself in you, like Narcissus drowning, fooled by what he'd thought was real.

*

The last time I saw you was at your house on Iberville. I came over because you asked me to. I realize now that you were probably scared. You were losing yourself, you were so unhappy. I was numb. You stood against the wall and sank down to the floor. It was raining outside, and you were crying. “Please, can’t you just love me the way I am?”

As at every meeting, she was bringing together her imaginary idea of him (an incomparably better one, impossible in reality) with him as he was.

February 2022

52 Email Excerpts, 2014-2015

Erin Riedel

1. It's funny to me that you have buried your face between my legs numerous times but have never seen the winter coat I wear almost every day. I'm glad you liked it.

2. You seemed troubled when I saw you, maybe just about your bus passes. I find I can usually sense when something is off with you, and it seemed to be today.

3. Have we totally given up on trying to be chaste while you're my supervisor?

4. If you ever need time away from me to figure out your marriage stuff, I will respect that. If you decide to end things with me to work on your marriage, I will respect that.

5. I think you should take a job in Middle-of-Nowhere, KY, and I will move with you to a big dumpy farmhouse, and I'll work on my novel and have a big garden and cook you delicious foods.

6. I'm glad you weren't too freaked out by the dongs. I had forgotten there were dongs in there. Your dong is my favorite dong, both on its own merits and because it's attached to someone so sexy.

7. If you were my boyfriend, I would have let you cut the grass while I worked in the garden, and then we would have taken a shower, and then if we had any energy left we would have had slow lazy sex, and then taken a nap, and then gone for frozen yogurt, and then grilled something delicious for dinner and eaten on the patio.

8. I hope you are not buying into stereotypes about the perceived lack of masculinity of Asian men. (I also hope you'll start using the word Asian instead of oriental.)

9. It was mostly rumors, though your lovesick tweeting didn't help.

10. You are so full of crap. That's not generally something I'd say about you, but about this particular issue, you totally are.

11. If it bothers you that I still don't believe you 100%, ask yourself how I possibly could when our relationship is only able to exist because you're such a good liar.

12. With each passing day, I grow angrier and more resentful.

13. It sounds like your thoughts about the future are solidifying to some extent, and while I'm trying not to get my hopes up, I do hope that the future involves your dick in me. A lot.

14. I'm sorry if my strong opinions are inappropriate, but this shit pisses me off. Jesus.

15. Your hair is so beautiful. I was admiring it while you were going down on me (as I always do). It always startles me how absolutely perfect it is. And I don't mean how it's styled, I mean the hair itself.

16. You should say goodbye when you end a text conversation. It's good etiquette. Not every text exchange, but every situation in which someone's trying to converse with you.

17. I want to be utterly yours. Yes, yes, precautions and caveats, uncertainty, either of us could walk away at any time. But I am so devoted to you and so hopelessly in love with you.

18. Please tread lightly on my heart. It is so tender for you.

19. I certainly hope we are able to start spending more time together soon. This once-a-week shit is for the birds, though I am trying to be patient.

20. I'm sorry I was whiny and cranky last night. I was disappointed that at first you seemed into it and then had a bunch of reasons why you weren't.

21. I understand that we need to continue to employ some level of discretion in our relationship, but it's hard. It's hard that I have no control over anything and that everything has to be on your terms.

22. I continue to find it odd that you virtually never talk about the future with me, which I think makes it harder for me to be patient, because I don't have a sense of what it is that I'm even waiting for. I mean, what's it going to be like? All you ever do is warn me about how you're old and infirm and boring.

23. Of course I'm going to hang with it until we're free of our previous relationships. I understand that we're in a complicated transitional period. I'm not going anywhere.

24. I really do understand and appreciate your desire to take things one day at a time.

25. The world is an amazing place that is far too vast to be experienced in a single lifetime. I am so eager to figure out what little piece of it we're going to experience together.

26. I dreamed I was riding your cock last night. 😊

27. I keep thinking about our shared orgasm and getting turned on again. And the second go-round was so hot. I felt you getting hard again but thought you'd be too tired to do anything with it, and the next thing I knew you were inside me.

28. I miss you terribly, but I don't feel like you're emotionally starving me, don't worry.

29. Janis left me a voicemail inviting me to sign your Boss's Day Card and said, "I know you're very fond of him." Ha!

30. But at the same time things have been weighing on me lately and tonight they got really heavy.

31. I think I sort of fake being decently adjusted to most people, but once you get to know me, as you know, I'm actually kind of a mess. And deep down at my core I am full of shame and believe that I am inherently unlovable.

32. Sometimes I feel so broken and alone. I wonder why I did not end up happily married and making babies, why my life sometimes feels like a booby prize.

33. I am not mad at you about anything, but I am so frustrated by this situation and the endless waiting.

34. I know it is not your intent, but I often feel wrong for wanting to spend time with you, wrong for wanting talk about the future with you, wrong for wanting to daydream with you, wrong for wanting you as much as I do.

35. You undo me, and I want to give myself over to it, but I can't. I am unsure if you will ever allow yourself to be undone by anyone again.

36. I am sorry for this gigantic, rambling, pathetic email.

37. I think you will find me to be lower maintenance than expected once we're in a regular relationship.

38. The Ronnie photo was meant to be shitty. I was drunk and angry. I have told you that I absolutely can't stand the silent treatment, but you do it anyway.

39. You told Brian that our relationship isn't serious and admitted to me that you're ashamed of it. I don't know what to do with that information.

40. You've said you don't want to think too much about our relationship because if you do, you'll realize it's a bad idea. How can you expect me to feel secure or valued or to be patient under those conditions?

41. Over the past month or so, I have reminded myself over and over and over again to keep opening my heart, wider and wider, even when it's counterintuitive, even when it frightens me.

42. Time after time, I am reminded that I am never the most important thing, not even sometimes, that I am only ever entitled to your leftovers.

43. You want my unconditional love, and I try my damnedest to give it to you, but you won't acknowledge me as your girlfriend, even between us, even to yourself.

44. This is like some kind of bizarre unpaid relationship internship, in which I do all of the stuff a girlfriend does but don't get any actual recognition.

45. I have been cutting you slack for almost two years. I am always being told to wait.

46. You refuse to define our relationship, but you want to continue to reap its benefits. I am simply unwilling to continue with this arrangement.

47. I can no longer play a role in your deluding yourself about the type of person you are.

48. You don't get to keep doing something that you claim to find morally objectionable and then tell yourself that you're not really doing it.

49. I don't know what else to say to you.

50. I don't believe what I want from you is unreasonable.

51. I have tried to meet you so much more than halfway, and it hasn't mattered.

52. You will never know how profoundly I love you and how much this breaks my heart.

April 2022

Thaumatrope

Kristine Langley Mahler

Power dream

I meet him again at a party or a reunion; whatever it is, I know we are supposed to be meeting like this—publicly, after all these years. We are being honored at the event simply for being who we are, or were. The onlookers indicate the only way we can show them we understand that gift is to kiss one another. The tension is terrible and wonderful because, after all, the tension is my favorite part. I do not want to actually kiss him. I want to be poised forever in the moment where we both know we are about to kiss, where I retain some semblance of control.

The dream of fantasy

The basement is cluttered with people. The walls are cinder-block, the floor is cement, dark corners lurk everywhere, full of bodies. My boyfriend is over there. We are moving in together in three months. But I address a nearby boy, which is strange since I typically do not talk to people I don't know. Something is settled so I can be who I am not. The boy speaks in hipster clichés about the time he drove to Colorado, how he picked up some new album on vinyl, the trite tripe I insult outside of this basement. I listen like I'm hearing it for the first time, which I suppose I am. I'm riveted by how much he believes in his performance, how certain he is that my interest is authentic. He maintains constant eye contact, and I pretend I am taking him very, very, seriously, though I am seriously rude, questioning everything he says and asking for explanations like I'm a decade older. I might as well be. I am moving toward an apartment in Omaha, Nebraska with a dishwasher, off-street parking, a job with retirement benefits. This boy is telling me he might go check out "Portland, Arrigan." Later, my boyfriend accuses me of flirting with the boy, but I do not know how to say that I couldn't stop egging him on. I couldn't walk away from someone who wanted to convince me.

Restraint dream

I arrive at his house. Actually, it is his parents' house, because while I know where he really lives now, the Google Maps screenshot has not fixed itself deep enough in my subconscious. So I substitute the house in which I knew him. I am in town with my own family, finally doing what he proposed by email fifteen years ago—stopping to visit on my way somewhere else. He has a wife, or a girlfriend, but she is not there. Neither is my husband. My children evaporate once I get inside his parents' house and his mother greets me. My children were a ruse to show him that there was no strange intent on my part; I would never do something inappropriate in front of them. He looks inordinately pleased.

The dream of acknowledgment

He asks, "Which bitch is which?" We are clustered around a swing on the playground, whirling above the sawdust, someone's legs tucked tight in a tire, body bent inward to increase the centrifugal speed. Someone is hurtling in orbit and someone else is pushing, keeping the rotation intact. There is no question he knows which bitch is which; we have been in the same elementary school for the last five years. Bitch does not sting, because I'm not sure it's a slur. That word's supposed to be as bad as *fuck*, as bad as *shit*, but I think it's like saying *hot damn*. I am just grateful he has bothered to address me.

Confession dream

This is the confrontation for which I have been preparing over the last twenty years. The veil lifts on the two of us alone somewhere, and my limbs lighten like they did when I used to imagine him surprising me by showing up in my town. He has shown up after all. I want to kiss him so badly I can barely hold myself together. I am desperate to see if we still know each other's mouths all these years later—to see if we had imprinted something vital upon each other when we taught each other how to kiss. But I do not. Somehow I know that by refusing to fulfill desire, I can keep it alive. Instead, I look at him and I am overcome with warmth. My tongue loosens and I tell him—not indirectly tell a friend, not write a Livejournal, not allude in an email quiz, not obfuscate in song lyrics appended to a message—how much I loved him. How long I loved him. To ventilate those feelings, to see his face soften, feels like all I have ever wanted. The thaumatrope spool untwists and hurtles forward, then backward, then forward. I make him approach me. I make him recede.

The dream of correction

He does not like me. He likes me, but he doesn't like me like that. He has liked every other girl in our large friend group "like that," regardless of their availability. My lack of desirability allows me to talk to him without worrying that he's taking it the wrong way, but I also put on more mascara. I have a boyfriend, and I do not want to trade him in—I'm not even attracted to my friend—but I also do not want to be the only girl excluded from this free-for-all. He will not stay in a room alone with me. He finds a reason to leave when I arrive. I sequester our friends and whisper at them, *I don't know why he doesn't like me*, alluding to situation after situation, hoping someone will suggest *maybe he is avoiding you because you are the one he likes the most.* Nobody does. But I catalog avoidance as potential, and I dream of power.

May 2022

Negative Space

Alyson Zetta Williams

1.

I would need to be held, I think. The photo shows *The Calling of St. Matthew* hanging adjacent to the equally-as-devastating Caravaggios, *St. Matthew and the Angel* and *The Martyrdom of St. Matthew* inside Rome's Contarelli Chapel. I search *caravaggio contarelli chapel* at least once a week and shiver every time. It's the middle of summer. My self-guided tour is the same: first the photo taken from around the corner of the room in which they hang, then the photo with the reverent upward angle. Then, under incandescent lighting, the photo that directly confronts *St. Matthew and the Angel,* the two others on either side pointing towards it like path and destination. Around Matthew and the angel, lit so serenely, is no shadow, no gradient, the most blunt confrontation of the void out of the three. So much of it to fall into. The intense light of meeting a higher power requires so much inverse darkness. I would need to be held, but how to hold what is not there?

No one paints nothing like Caravaggio. The space around his subjects is a subject itself. That beyond-black presence—the nothing around something—has never been so rich. The negative space. For something not there, it is formidably instructive. As with most things that *aren't,* there is the drive to fill negative space with *is.* Negative space is design. It defines the relationship of one element to another. It is the limit of the subject. It is where a painting breathes. It is storing every possibility. It is where fantasy occurs.

It wasn't until my first term of art school that I was able to practice drawing from a live model. I had only drawn from static, unfatigued figures in magazine editorials and ads. *Draw the space around them,* the professor would instruct during a longer pose. *If you cannot draw the hand, draw the space around the hand.* The paper is now a shadow.

Continuing to confuse chiaroscuro with negative space. Even the name for my own abscess is elusive. Negative space being the space absent of subject, chiaroscuro being the darkness in value of that absence of subject, the darkness of the space without. There is, apparently, a compromise. *While tenebrism developed from chiaroscuro, unlike that technique, it did not strive for greater three-dimensionality, but was compositional, using deep darkness as a kind of negative space.*

Everything in my room has so much to say: blanket folds, pillowcase wrinkles, lines created by the shirts on my bed. Life has leaked from me, infused them. I cannot feel my lines. Hard to feel without someone tracing them. Sex is like my name being told to me repeatedly, except one quickly irritates, except one I am able to remember. Concentrate on the feeling of you not touching me. It feels like the heat of the lamp, casting values across me that would, when drawn, reveal the lines I cannot feel.

What came first: the dark or the light? The negative or positive value? My mother told me from a young age: *there's some hole in you.* An accusation, but I felt it too. I did not consider the hole an open secret. Just open. Is increased invisibility not the privilege of a hole? Did I start writing because of the hole, or did I write the hole into me? Out of me, whatever was there before. At some point, it must have occurred to stop trying to fill it, to empty whatever was left inside. The closest I could get to doing something about it.

The amnesia of your absence: did you ever exist at all? I read your messages to prove you were once there, thinking of me, here. I consider going to the grocery store and wonder if that's real, either. It takes me a moment to understand that someone is looking at me, when they are. My slow recognition probably looks like a stare, like I want something I don't, or am not supposed to want. People tell me I'm tall, sometimes strangers, and I come to realize that *You're* bothers me more than *tall.* Tall like an indictment. It feels less and less like something I command, or *are,* reminding me of all of me I no longer stick to. Phantom inches. You asked me my height the second time you called, said all the same things. Talking on the phone leaves the body behind; a satellite. An imagined wire will host you now. Your voice is taller than me. I only need to feel myself to the extent that my back is against the wall, my hand holding the phone.

2.

I want to call it eerie, that thing I recognize in Caravaggio's paintings. Eerie: a situation where something is either too missing or too present, within the scene's generally understood context. He often accomplishes both at once. I retreat from the glistening figure emerging from the darkness around it. Is it an evil in me startled by what is alive and colorful? Blank black space: a mythological creature with an unknown lore.

This book is an artwork unto itself, reads the art book's favorite review. I lift the first page of a tucked away three-paneled print of *The Calling of St. Matthew* only to quickly collapse the panels again at the first sight of utter blackness that is the top left corner. Darkness shrouds Jesus, his halo nearly severed by the split of shadow and light. He points at Matthew; the light points at Matthew; Matthew points at himself. Both are cast by God: the light thrown and the tax collector invited into apostleship. The splintering light that is your higher power requires so much inverse darkness.

When I describe my negative space, I call it *a non-subject area.* Darkness and blackness have been called upon so often to describe this that they have seeped into subjectivity, escaping their original function of obscurity. Is this success—becoming light and line? The void is a meme. Dark, *the dark,* is a destination too often used by my mother and others who can't elaborate on what *the dark* looks like, why it occurs, and why I shouldn't become it.

I sleep with you, negatively speaking. Which is to say you sleep, and I lie curling in positions around you. Forced to live through the night like I was made of it. You smile in the morning as though one of us is not more acquainted with night than the other. Metaphor: will I ever join you in normalcy, subjecthood, sleep? I had closed my eyes, saw the colors, believed it was happening. There's no better way to illustrate everything else about you and me.

If what is negative is forgotten, then the positive is what has been forgotten to be forgotten. The subject may exist to give shape to the nothing around it. How many times did I believe I loved someone when I actually loved the shape the world took around them? The way everything else appeared when forced to accommodate their space in the frame? I loved being the substance moving through the world in the shape of their silhouette.

I became better at acting than saying. Subtle, sculpted manipulations were my ways of speaking without having to say anything. At least, not what I wanted to say. At least, not what would bring me into the light. My speech jagged, cut in parts. To fragment feels virtuous, a dispersing of myself into others so as not to be a selfish whole.

(A selfish hole).

In our triptych—me, you, and the space between—I can't remember who the light cast down on. It's easier to add dark value than it is to erase it.

3.

I can only look at the paintings in the book during daylight hours. Something about all that empty space in the dark is threatening when I haven't created it myself.

The tarot reading my friend gives is somewhat grave. We smoke half a joint, and she's pulling cards and making faces and telling me what they mean. High, I've never been paranoid about anything happening inside of me. Only what's on the outside. Only how the inside translates to the outside. It's not that she's revealed the death card; I know enough to know the reaper catalyzes change within life as well as outside it. She puts her hand over another card and looks at me with eyes that either suck everything out of me or push all of her into me. We're both seeing some of me in the light for the first time. I'm the friend in the movie you lose to paranormal activity. I know how that character, afforded so little point of view, feels before they're turned inside out by the hungry, nothing entity. I want to accuse her of trying to scare me in a sleepover way but see that, really, her eyes aren't asking anything of me. They're just seeing.

In the rooms where paintings hang, we are the negative space.

Judith somewhat timidly slays Holofernes on the book's pages before me. Her seduction successful, he is the one left bleeding out after having pillaged her town. He is captured forever in the moment we all count on ending quickly. In one still scene, Holofernes is halfway decapitated, turned toward Judith in a moment of realizing his fate and agony—there is no mistaking that the mouth agape could mean anything else. Still, he is beautiful, his skin a living ochre. Death: as long as there are still words to stick to it—"imminent," perhaps—is worthy of lighting. Suffering to the front. Retreating into the nothing-space is cowardly; bolder than execution, bolder than executing, is the choice to act. The void background has yet to overcome them, any of them, though a shadow starts to dim Holofernes's face. In his forever agony, a hint of time passing. Is he exhibiting terror or ecstasy, the shadow finally engulfing him?

July 3rd: *I don't necessarily hate or dislike him for how things ended. His near disappearance is now a certain disappearance. Now that the anxiety has passed, the uncertainty of his remaining a subject, I've found relief on the other side, I can only sit and have a tiny lament over crossing paths with someone in the light.*

4.

The online magazine has chosen *Self-Portrait as the Sick Bacchus* to accompany the short article discussing Caravaggio's light. Four pages available for printing, and one is fully occupied by *Bacchus.* The figure, painted in ill tones of green and yellow, resists becoming the black nothing behind it. It will be a lot of ink; my printer can do it. A paper slick and black sliding onto the tray; can I do it? If Caravaggio-as-Bacchus is sick, does this make the void a compassionate one? For once, it is easier to look into the dark when forced to choose between it and the rotten figure. You know things are grave when Caravaggio, whose figures usually writhe in warmth, uses an outright blue tone in the body.

I'll fade to black and disappear of my own accord. But there are times when I retreat into negative space only to enact the gravity of doing so. I pull you into me. You can't see the schemes taking place in the dark. I find images of Contarelli Chapel's interior from new, accidental-looking angles, the paintings somehow always in frame. What is this gravity the Caravaggios hold, and can you feel it, as someone who's never sought it?

[Caravaggio] achieved this effect with a limited palette typical of 17th-century painters: iron oxide colors (red ocher, yellow ocher, umber), a few mineral pigments (vermilion, lead-tin yellow, lead white), organic carbon black, and verdigris.

Allowing for light is what killed Caravaggio. Like much of his life, there is no official documentation of his death, though lead poisoning seems to be a comfortable theory for those who speculate. Lead white, predating zinc and titanium, contains exactly what its name suggests.

St. Matthew, too, sees his end in the light. Though his life begins again upon meeting Christ, so too his death. Receiving the light Caravaggio has cast first from an out-of-frame God, then from Jesus, Matthew's call to sainthood has a sequel in Caravaggio's *Martyrdom of Saint Matthew.* He worked on them simultaneously. Only the dead can be saints. Matthew must become one before the other. The darkness inherent to becoming an eternal light.

Richard Siken: *I have my body and you have yours. Believe it if you can. Negative space is silly.*

My writing is not toward myself. That would be frivolous; my goal is to dissipate into others, take up space in their little corners where they might find me later. One thing I do write to myself:

Stop believing in nothing until it is something. Stop believing that what is not there is more powerful than what is. I wake in the bed where

I changed shapes throughout the night assuming that my mere presence is the reason you no longer want me.

Living in negative space is desperate voyeurism. I think I am learning how to be until you, in the light, are gone, and all space is just space again.

A subject has boundaries; negative space is forever-shaped. If I end this essay with a period, I will have made something I can hold to the light, myself dissolving in it.

July 2024

The Nurse's Lament

Lexi Kent-Monning

The man I'm with tells me I'm a giver and he's a taker, that he won't be able to stop taking from me, so I should stop giving to him. He calls me a nurturer. He's the first person to call me this. It's the most immediate, identifiable trait of mine that others see, but I had no idea despite my three decades inhabiting the role.

I consider the evidence.

Within two hours of meeting my ex-husband, I was sewing a hole in his pants. I told this story for twelve years. I wore it like a crown. I wanted everyone to hear the sweetness of when we met and he needed something, and my helping hands were doing it for him before we even knew each other's last names.

When my friends' three-year-old daughter wakes up from her nap, I'm the first adult she sees when she walks out of her bedroom. She asks me to help her on the toilet. She runs to the kitchen to announce it to her parents: "She wiped my bottom!" They redden, embarrassed, before instructing her to thank me and telling me I didn't have to help. It didn't occur to me that I didn't have to do it. I'd been mortified that I wasn't thinking a step ahead to assist when she first stumbled into the bathroom.

For years, I made nurturing my career. I took care of famous women, famous millionaires. They needed help with scheduling, picking up dry cleaning, pumping gas, grocery shopping, wrapping gifts, remembering to eat. They had access to everything in the world, but what they actually needed was a comrade, a peanut gallery, a friend who couldn't leave until they were told. Years later, I still dream of assuaging their anxieties. I wake up wishing I could have done more for them, remembering when I couldn't shield them from their own self-esteem, their insular disadvantages, their incredibly specific circumstances.

The nurturers never become the nurtured. When we need it, it doesn't come. I need it now, but nobody knows what to do. They love to tell me how strong I am, as though staying alive is so brave. If I choose the alternative, does that make me weak or scared or whatever the opposite is of brave? But there is no choice. I don't choose to be brave or strong. And I don't feel any of those traits I'm being assigned. Gravity pulls harder every day, though more often now, it feels like I'm being pushed towards the ground instead of pulled.

When I had someone, people always asked how he was first before asking me, "How are you?" Now that I'm alone and have no partner for them to ask me about, they instead start conversations with "My coworker is getting divorced," as if it's the only way to relate to me anymore. As if it's the totality of who I am now. They skip the how-are-yous altogether. Nobody wants to be near someone that makes them unsure of whether this could happen to them. If I mention my ex-husband, they become visibly tense, like I should know we don't speak of the living dead.

Loneliness is a necessary alienation. I can't face anyone when I don't know what to tell them, admit what's happening, or say it out loud. And now days go by when the only humans I interact with are ghost hands waving through windshields as neighbors drive past me. The glare on the glass makes it impossible to see their faces. I crave smelling my dog's breath because it's the only scent that belongs to someone else.

Last night, I dreamt a mountain lion stalked into a room I was lying down in, its tail whipping devilishly, erratically. It laid down behind me and put its head on my neck. I should have been scared, but I was so grateful to be touched that I didn't have any fear.

I feel others on my body in different places. It takes time for me to learn who it is. I feel my ex-husband in my sinuses. I feel The Taker in my eyes, my breath, and my fingers. What good is my body if not a shrine to those I love? A vessel for their needs and desires, a sacrifice for their woes and pains. My body becomes a decorated tomb, with marks to, for, by, and because of those I've loved.

I receive gifts of bubble bath, creams and oils, spa gift cards. As though the creams and oils are a cure-all salve for more than wrinkles.

I accept the gifts with performances of gratitude, dutifully carrying an open heart and mind as I use them. The massages end every single time with me in tears. My body, this shrine to those I love, can't accept this one-way touch, directed solely towards me. There's not an exchange, so it feels foreign and mistaken.

It's a dangerous hobby, keeping track of others. Knowing them better than they know themselves, better than you know yourself. Intellectually I know this: don't keep people as hobbies. Keep them as friends and lovers. Don't keep strange things, like a piece of rubber from the sole of my ex-husband's shoe that lives on my nightstand, or the list of things that make The Taker do a little dance. Let some things happen without keeping a record. Without turning it into your possession.

Months after my ex-husband leaves, the cobbler at the shoe repair stand eventually asks, tenderly, "Not married anymore?" as he rings up my pair of boots he's fixed.

"Not anymore," I affirm, matching his tone. "How did you know?"

"You stopped bringing his shoes and belts to fix."

Don't fix their things. Let them fix their own things.

June 2023

THE BODY

A Brief History of My Knees

Donna Vorreyer

I did not really have them as a baby. No bone, all cartilage, flexible to exit the womb, to wobble and fall without breaking. Pure articulation. Each knock or bump promptly kissed better, twin pom poms, soft and freckled. I was two, three, six perhaps, before the caps hardened to bone. Before they met the unmalleable world.

*

We were not allowed to ride bikes in the cemetery, so of course we rode our bikes directly to the cemetery. There was no traffic there, the streets paved and good for racing, and behind it? The construction site for a warehouse, one that had left a hill of displaced dirt about fifteen feet high. Slopes gentle enough to walk up but steep enough to speed down. We had named it Devil's Hill. The older kids took turns, gathering velocity with glee. When it was my turn, I made it all the way to the bottom, but the wheels slid out as I braked, and I crashed onto my left knee, scraping off a large patch of skin. Gravel and loose dirt mixed with blood. We wiped the wound the best we could with leaves and grass before making our way home. I headed straight to the bathroom, rinsed it, tried not to touch the raw and tender skin. I slapped on a Band-Aid, figuring if no one saw it, I wouldn't get in trouble. I took care to keep the bandage on through baths and changes of clothes, but I couldn't avoid favoring that leg, and when my father removed the bandage, the wound bloomed with green pus. He wasn't angry, but he told me he had to clean it, and it was going to hurt. He was not wrong, the peroxide plunging its needles into the wound and peaking into white foam.

*

I was always on the move as a teen, and my knees were a wonder. They danced. They flipped off diving boards. They crouched to hide behind bushes when the police drove by the park where we drank beer. They ran around softball diamonds, turning and diving to grab line drives down the third base line. They shivered when boys laid hands on their bare curves, peeking out from my uniform skirt. Oil-shot, fluid. Bliss hinges. Bruised and tender fruit, the kind whose battering makes them sweeter.

*

Axis. Bend. Bond. Bracket. Bridge. Connection. Copula. Coupling. Crux. Elbow. Hook. Joint. Juncture. Link. Pin. Spring. Swivel. Unity. Vinculum.

*

I started to run in my twenties. I completed my first marathon at twenty-nine, and I continued throughout my thirties and forties. No race was easy, and none were pretty. The last marathon involved hours of tears and, upon finishing, crawling into a hotel bed with bleeding feet and ice packs tied to my knees with towels. My knees still handle workout stress in various ways. One knee gets stuck in position if I don't move it enough, and I cup a hand over the top as if to cradle the pain, like catching water from a pump. They swell, and I ice them. They pop, and I rest them. RICE, RICE, baby.

*

Nemeses of the clumsy: Coffee table corners. Uneven sidewalks. My own feet. Hems of flared yoga pants. Hidden divots in gravel or grass. Deep stairs. Worn stone stairs. Wet stairs. Stairs in general. Midwestern winter parking lots. The knees are the first responders of the clumsy, heroes bearing the brunt of each misstep. Little turtle shells. Little armadillos.

*

The closest they have come to a serious injury was a torn meniscus at age fifty-five. Not from some feat of athleticism or bravery, but from walking my dog when he stopped and stiffened and turned me two directions at once. The doctor pointed out the minor tear and evidence of significant arthritis, explained that surgery wasn't warranted, suggested rest and low-impact exercise. It was all a bit anticlimactic. After years of being told my knee pain was nothing, I was expecting a revelation. As it turns out, they are simply imperfect, things that I depend upon despite their flaws, like a car that has no heat and a door that won't open, but still starts and gets you where you need to go.

*

Pop and lock. Buckle and twist. Contort and hyperextend. The therapist says lunges and squats. Cobblers and figure fours. Dead bugs and happy babies. Clamshells and step ups. Deadlifts and foam rollers. *No burpees,* says the orthopedist. *They keep me in business.*

January 2022

Practice

Erin Dorney

All of the steps I have to go through before doing yoga on my mother's kitchen floor: convince her, move furniture, vacuum, assure the dogs it's fine. Then, listen to her knees crack as she rolls around by my side, a sixty-eight-year-old roly poly bug, pill in pink pajamas. We love the same poses. *I used to be able to do this,* she tells me.

We lie flat together. As the video transitions to an advertisement for healthier water, she says *this is so good.* Tomorrow we will move to the carpet in the basement, in front of the gas fireplace, since her yoga mat is so thin. I try to keep from moving until the five minutes have passed—still haven't heard a snowplow. In corpse pose, I notice all the dust we missed, in the corners, under her Christmas tree. The dogs still don't understand, licking our faces, biting our hands.

No one tells you about exercising with the elderly. I hide inside the hood of my sweatshirt as it falls over my face. I leave my hair in front of my eyes so I don't have to see what she's doing. Somehow our bodies used to fit one inside the other—two nesting dolls. Now, we are almost equal-sized lumps, windshield wipering our knees into one another like flacid battering rams. She will keep getting smaller while I keep getting larger. I would keep her safe inside me if I could.

*

I like when my mom says *oh fuckey* when we're doing yoga together. It usually means she's about to tip over. During relaxation, she flicks my finger—a six-foot-tall gnat buzzing at my side. I try to tickle her armpit, but jokes on me, she says—she lost all feeling on that side after her surgery.

I try not to go shirtless in my mom's house. I feel sad that I have two breasts when she only has one, while at the same time, I wish that I had none, while at the same time I wish none of it felt like such a big deal or even something worth taking note of. There's a round Band-Aid stuck to the inside of her shower curtain liner. It's been there for four years.

I imagine someone peeking inside the basement window of her split level. She is watching television in front of the fire alone. She is collecting the biggest pinecones I have ever seen. She is arranging rescued blue glass bottles from tallest to largest, all of them leading down, down, down, to a framed photograph of my youngest brother in diapers on a beach.

It is snowing where I am with her, but it's warmer than where I usually live. This feels like a treat—the sun—until I feel whiplash on my face from wind across the open fields. I wanted to say where I normally live, but nothing is normal now, including the fact of my being here. Last time, the only thing I wanted was to be with her. Now, it's happening again, and here I am, unfolding each day like brittle paper.

*

The dogs go wild when we do yoga. They are on the floor with us, biting our hair, between our hands when we bow down. We shout, they bark, and Adriene smiles on the flatscreen—oblivious. My mom thanks her for anticipating her soreness, and I see how easily a relationship begins.

My mom wonders why I lock the bathroom door behind me. I wonder why she keeps a bar of soap in a dish filled with cloudy water, so soft that it collapses in my hand when I try to grab it—solid only to sight.

When the practice ends, my mom looks down at me. I can see up her nightgown—thrifted, with another woman's name scrawled across the tag. She asks what I am doing. *Yoga*, I say. I am incredulous, while also knowing that the odds are high that one day I will open a door and ask her what she is doing. And she will not answer.

The floor itself will have no significance to most readers unless I say this: It is where they found my uncle, body crumpled, days later. I want to say that his was the first body I ever saw dying, but they're around me every day. We all know this—my mom, Adriene, me, the dogs nipping at our fingers—but somehow still, we practice.

*

Practice. Act. Pace. Race. Ice. Pact. Pie. Pit. Price. Pat.

My mom says *blah blah blah* to the screen, then tips over. Each time we forward fold, I check for Covid toes. *Should J come over?* she asks. This could mean three different people, and I want none of them in our space. This cold basement—these layers of carpet, mat, blanket for her knees. I could make a study of the songs she sings herself. I could stay another week.

*

A list of things my mother has given me during week one of the second pandemic winter: terra cotta bird-feeder, vintage refrigerator jar, wool socks, boot cleats, my grandmother's birdwatching book (after dragging it out from the garbage and brushing coffee grounds off the cover), waterproof baby books for bath time.

She's tried to give me other things, but I can't bear to think of her living alone in the house without them. I only said I liked them because I want her to know that I love being here.

She doesn't think we worked hard enough yesterday. She *wasn't tired enough to fall asleep.* So today we will walk along the salt-slicked road, and she will tell me about all her neighbors. Then, we will ready the house, but I don't want to think about what for.

*

I hope she knows I'm suffering, my mom says, standing with her hand on the kitchen island while we drink our first cups of coffee and count each limb the wind knocked down. But later I'm the one swearing at the screen while I jam my hips into the floor. *What season was this filmed?* I ask, as I look outside and tell myself—again—that time does not exist. How could it, when each morning I meet a new person, another self I still have time to be.

*

J watches us on our "yoga papers" and then wants to show us how the bridge goes up and down—a real happy baby. I don't want her to remember this as women working out, so I tell her we are getting strong. We are feeling good. She doesn't want to do it unless it's on the list, so we write it down and cross it out. Also on the list: Snow angels, make pizza with grandma, read. It seems like I'm picking the most poetic things, but I'm not, the whole list is like this, I swear—stickers, walk the dogs, paint rocks with Aunt Erin.

I show her how to roll the mat, then explain how I am going upstairs to write my next book. Kids can learn anything fast, anything you show them.

Today my mom said *I'm glad she knows how I feel,* and asked me to put yoga on her phone for the upcoming vacation. Of course I am hatching more plans—daily check-ins, encouraging texts, quizzes about what Adriene said that day to see if she's keeping up. She can already do more scissor kicks than day one. She can already navigate to the next video on her own.

*

It's seven days later, and I can't find the face again—the one I saw in my mom's popcorn ceiling.

*

Today before yoga, I was almost squashed by a 90-inch cabinet. The neighbor and I both bloodied. Before admitting defeat, I reminded her that there was a smear of red across her face—no one should pick up their kids in that state. I still have trouble keeping my own face soft.

In Florida, my mom & L roll back the rug, clear the living room to work out together before they hit the beach. *It feels safer than the exercise room,* she says. I can't imagine either of them doing any move correctly, but I guess that is the point of practice. L likes the sound of Adriene's voice, so I tell her about the meditation series. Personally, I feel like there's something to be written about how she softens herself over time, becomes more palatable for us—prettier, stronger, better outfits—tries to assert more control over her vocal chords.

But some of my favorite moments are when that all slips away. When Adriene is tongue-tied, or fucks up, or fucks up then mentions that she just fucked up. Or sings, or smears "something" across her belly, when surely we all know what "something" could mean.

*

I want the washing away of every broken stick, dog shit pile, salty muck sloughed off the road. I want to watch through my window, surrounded by books, flakes fall against the balsam firs. And every hour, I want to move the car and shovel until I sweat right through my shirt. This poem is a prayer in which I conjure the second Monday of a brand new year. In this essay I will.

I want you to know I was here, but I just have nothing to say. I feel lucky, but also like I want to cut the too-tight ends of my sweatpants right off. Does age recalibrate? I don't want to be anyone-else-absorbed—a sun that fades in and out instead of going up and down.

*

Can you believe there are just things in the sky? my mother asks me, as we stand by the French doors looking out over the lawn. *Up there, existing.* I focus on scuffing up the floor so she won't slip when I leave.

The morning she left for her mastectomy, I crouched inside a dugout behind my mother's house. I wept as fog lifted over the field. She returned to me in pieces, and even then, the worst days were still to come. At the good spot, we search the beach for heart-shaped rocks to bring home for J. My mom shows me her pile, asks me *do you think they're good enough? Perfect,* I say, to every twisted, weathered, smoothed-over stone.

September 2023

Mirror Moments

Sabrina Small

I first see Anne Hathaway's shoulders in the Amazon romcom, *The Idea of You,* just before the two leads have their first kiss. She's wearing an oversized vintage blazer paired with a bohemian skirt and heeled booties. It's a specific embodiment of Laurel Canyon chic, and it's aspirational in all the ways that serve my demographic (artsy middle-aged moms). It's the outfit of a woman who strolls through life without haste or hunger.

And then she takes the blazer off.

You see, it's hot in the Glendale studio where she's showing art to Nicholas Galitzine, the boy-band hunk that recently fell into her charmingly chaotic life. It's so hot that she takes her blazer off and must reveal her birdlike clavicle, arms and shoulders. They seem to float above her electric blue tube-top in a disturbingly disembodied way.

My LA-trained brain does the math. I know that if she looks this thin on screen, she looks at least ten pounds thinner in person, and I know exactly what that looks like.

I get obsessed with *The Idea of You*. I watch it on my laptop in bed in Berlin and text with my sisters in LA about how skinny Anne Hathaway looks. We dissect her wardrobe and her hair. We are harsh critics raised to be ruthless in our self-judgment as well. *The Idea of You* is a manual for our self-reflection. Each of us will project onto it differently. For me, the movie is about a single mom finding soul restorative love.

I've been on Hinge for three months after several years alone. I am newly queer and celibate and unsure how to proceed. I match with shy looking men and trans men. I am afraid of matching with anyone else. My first date is with an Italian who looks like a hipster version of Pacino. He spends most of our time together talking about how much he hates Germans and how hard it is raising his autistic son. At one point, I will rub his shoulders because he complains so bitterly about non-stop screen work. He's a videographer for a news agency, but he used to be an aspiring filmmaker. He name-drops Bruce La Bruce and tells me his short film from twenty years ago won an award at Cannes. When we split from each other at the edge of Goethe Park, I say, "see you soon," and he says, "We'll see." I realize the next day, going over it, that he never asked me a single question.

I spend a lot of time looking in the mirror and wondering if anyone I'm attracted to will ever be attracted to me. I am sixty pounds overweight by LA standards. My clavicle is meaty and sun-damaged. My neck has moles and skin tags and wild hairs sprouting out of fat folds. My shoulders are broad, hunched, and masculine.

I want to be Anne Hathaway. I want to be in her body and flirt with Nicholas Galitzine. I want to be on set and hand my giant water bottle to an assistant and be so thin that it makes children uncomfortable. I want to fall in love with a British boy band superstar. I want to live in a world where these exaggerated power dynamics are plausible, where my age and his fame have brought both of us world weary wisdom.

There is a scene halfway through the film that breaks into my fantasy and fills me with contempt. Anne Hathaway and her beaux are gallivanting around Europe for his tour, and they rent a house in the south of France with a cadre of twenty-somethings. Anne spies the group by the pool. She clocks the young hotties in their bikinis and decides to change out of her bikini into a more demure one-piece. She stands before the mirror and cups her breasts mimicking fullness and lets them fall flat again. She looks supernaturally beautiful, but she is pretending to be searching for flaws.

Fuck Anne Hathaway and her lowland sad eyes and her faux insecure lip biting and her bird shoulders. You broke the fourth wall, bitch. I can buy the meet-cute in a trailer bathroom, the success of her "inclusive" Silver Lake gallery space, and even the post-sex lip-sync to *Dance Hall Days*. But I can't buy this self-conscious mirror moment.

At that moment, I left the film and started thinking about the director, Michael Showalter. He used to be on MTV's *The State,* which shaped me deeply. I had a crush on him. He was thin, and his nose was amazing. Later on, he got fat. He carried his weight like an addict, like someone actively losing their battle with self-destruction. I wonder what it was like for him to shoot this scene. Was he telling Anne Hathway which parts of herself to point out as flaws? Was he thinking about his own experience facing the mirror?

I matched with an Egyptian in his mid-thirties. He is a financial auditor, but he dreams of being a porn star. It's hard to tell in our brief chat if he's joking or serious. He's not that cute in his pictures, but I want to see if there's banter. If there's banter, maybe I can get more excited about meeting him. Our chat keeps coming back to the porn thing, and I don't feel comfortable meeting him. My sexuality is a tight complex knot in my solar plexus. Best case scenario—best case—I meet someone who adores me and is extremely patient and is willing to spend months helping me overcome trauma until I feel ready to be intimate. The Egyptian porn star won't ever be that person, so when he asks me on a date, I text back, "I think we have different appetites but good luck." He writes back a few minutes later. I read the words a few times without really absorbing what they say.

"It's cool. I thought I'd give dry old meat a try but I'm gonna stick to fresh young peaches."

I delete him and report his behavior as inappropriate to Hinge. I've never had to do that before. I questioned whether to do it at all. Maybe I'm overreacting—sticks and stones and so on—but I report him and Hinge sends an automated message saying they take safety seriously and then never follow up again.

In the movie *Civil War*, Kirsten Dunst plays a combat-hardened war photographer documenting the unfolding war in America. She's introduced in Cinéma vérité fashion, with no makeup or soft lighting. The camera makes no attempt to capture her best angle and seems, instead, to be intentionally capturing her worst angles, a'la Charlize Theron in *Monster*. Dunst appears grim, dead-eyed and weather-beaten. Her shoulders are hunched, and there's a dowager's hump in her back. She wears ill-fitting T-shirts and khakis. Her hair is pulled back from her jowly chin. She's really leaning into the ugly. I'm proud of her on our behalf. I know how far she's come. The darling of *The Virgin Suicides*, the sex symbol of sensitive, intellectual 90s teens; the hottie that smashed Jake Gyllenhaal and Garret Hedlund. She let herself age and harden.

Civil War is overwhelming and probably bad. I don't know. I wasn't really watching it. I was watching her and comparing myself to her and wondering if looking sort of like Kirstin Dunst in *Civil War* is good or bad. She looks like she doesn't give a fuck how she looks. On women, that can either read as badass or despairing.

There's a scene where Dunst and her posse enter a boutique in a safe zone, and she tries on a fancy green dress and gets her picture taken. It's not a movie where she's allowed to teleport the idea that she's self-critical because *It's fucking war people!* As far as I can tell, she's supposed to be thinking something like...These days of frivolity and dress-up are behind us and may never come back. The moment at the mirror is quickly overtaken by another photographer, a young female protege, who takes her mentor's picture and tells Dunst that she looks pretty when she smiles. It's a weird scene that is toying with flirtation but never makes a definitive choice. Still, I wonder whether there's a version of *Civil War* where Dunst has hot wartime sex with her protege? Whether there's an alternate reality where both Dunst and Hathaway get to experience spontaneous May/December romances?

None of this will matter in a year. Both of these actresses, who I studied as a girl and continue to study as an adult, will shed the skin of one film and enter another. It makes me feel grateful that my body is hidden. I don't have to watch myself on screen. I don't have to answer to fans who want me to stay the same. I can change quietly and hope that one day I'll be able to face my own image.

July 2024

Post-Op

Abigail Richards

I've got perfect little tits now—the kind that men write about in their protagonists' wet dreams. They're stiff and pale and peaked, the way recipes tell you your whipped cream should look so you know when to stop beating it.

A few days after the surgery, I lie on a thin sheet of paper as the doctor slithers the drains out from my underboob. The sensation nearly makes me pass out, but I force my eyes open, convinced I'm witnessing some vital life moment, like the birth of a child, that a later, more coherent version of me would surely not want to miss. I stare down. The boobs on my body are unrecognizable. Round and gravity-defying, my nipples stand in perfect salute, purple bruises spiraling out like pinch-thin petals. My scars sear their way down then under, two smiling cyclops, blood hanging like dull teeth. Anchor scars, they're called, which is funny because I've never felt lighter. My before-breasts were the anchors, really: diving off the sides of my body every time I lay down like they were the ones trying to jump ship. Now they jiggle stiffly like Jell-O just pulled from the fridge.

The doctor slicks the blood away and re-mummifies my chest. When I stand up off the table, I stumble, first steps taken off a boat onto dry land. I feel eighty pounds lighter and also like I still might pass out. I can't stop staring down.

They're so *small,* I marvel to the doctor as she peels her latex gloves off.

Well, she replies. They're not *that* small.

*

I remember when I first became aware of the problem. I was in my bedroom with my mom, pulling the thin material of a training bra over my chest. It stretched way more than it should, and we both noticed.

My mother was looking down at me resolutely.

Well, she said, looks like you're just going to be a bit bigger-chested.

I was twelve. Already I could feel it: that unnamable hot frustration. At the bra, at my body, at myself.

Is that a good thing or bad thing? I asked her.

Neither, she said, her back already turned to me. It's just you.

But when you're a kid, there can really only be good or bad. And she hadn't said good.

*

I was giddy to show the surgeon my boobs for the first time—it was like I was tattling on two troublesome bullies who were finally gonna get reprimanded. But when I took my shirt off at the first consultation, the surgeon was far more diplomatic than I'd hoped. Silent, she touched one drooping nipple with the tip of her pen. She gently lifted one boob up and let it plop back down.

Well, you've certainly got some asymmetry there, she said. But then said nothing else.

When you go in for a breast reduction consultation, they take a Sharpie and draw on your body where they'll make incisions. They draw a little circle around your nipple, and then another circle higher up to show where your nipple will go. A dotted line connects these two points like a border, dividing the hill of breast in half. It looks like one of those game plans that sports teams have on a whiteboard to show where everyone will go, to show how they will win.

After she'd drawn on me, the surgeon showed me before-and-after photos of surgery results, which all looked like mugshots except the women were shirtless and their heads were cropped off. The surgeon pointed at one and said, She's kinda like you—that's probably what yours will look like. I took a picture of it with my phone.

The next photo I had in my camera roll was of me in a red dress I was trying on for Valentine's Day. I liked the dress, but, as always, my boobs looked comically huge, jutting out too intensely from my body.

I got a thrill seeing those two pictures next to each other. I quickly scrolled back and forth, trying to blur the two images into one like a flipbook: me in dress, disembodied tits, me in dress, disembodied tits. It didn't really work, but it was nice to imagine.

Sharpie stays on for a long time. For weeks after my consultation, I saw phantom remnants of dark lines across my shock-white skin. I made no great effort to scrub it off. I kind of liked it. I kind of wanted it to stay on. It was like looking at blueprints for your house renovations. I wanted to remember what it was going to be, rather than what it was.

*

In the elementary school changing room, I learned to make myself a concave thing, standing facing the corner like I'd be punished. I perpetually wore a sweaty white tank top under my gym clothes so no one would have to see too much of me all at once.

I was always averting my eyes, but when I'd accidentally catch a glimpse of the other girls I was shocked—how were their shapes so fundamentally different from mine? So compact? Spaghetti straps resting effortlessly against gentle bone, while mine dug into my shoulder fat like strings on a ham. It was so easy for them to slip out of miniature lace bras, to stand facing everyone else, to share aerosol cans of deodorant. Their bodies so inoffensive. Were we even the same gender, really? Should I even be in here?

There was one other girl in my class who was bigger, too. Tall with bright red hair. She arrived panting to gym class a second before the bell rang because she changed in the second-floor bathroom and had to run all the way back down to the auditorium. Quicker that way, she told me once, breathlessly. I didn't believe her for a second. I was so mad I didn't think of it first.

*

While I was on the waitlist for my breast reduction, I started running.

I told people it was because I found it relaxing, which I did, but more importantly, I wanted to make my stomach flatter. That seemed to be the overarching purpose of every bodily alteration I attempted: Make It Flatter. Like I was an unsteady kid in a sandbox just trying to pat everything even again.

When I ran, I wore three sports bras to keep my breasts at bay. It was very painful, but I tried to convince myself it was beneficial somehow, like carrying small weights in your hands to increase resistance or whatever. This was not true, of course. There were no benefits. But sometimes it helped to pretend.

I ran on a big oval track near my house. In the late afternoon, if I rounded the corner at just the right time, sometimes the sun would fall behind me in such a way that for a moment my shadow looked like nothing more than a big pair of tits with legs. Just for a moment. And then I would straighten, and it would look like me again, but still, that image stayed with me. For a moment, that was what I looked like. That was all I saw of myself.

I got the email in September one morning while I was approaching the track.

Hi Abby. I just wanted to let you know that you have been approved for your breast reduction surgery. I have some dates left in November and December if you wish to have it done shortly.

I stopped and squatted down in the grass with my hand against my mouth. In front of me, my shadow was only a circle, a tightly wound ball full of energy and possibility ready to explode like a planet or a big star. I stayed like that for a long time. I sucked tears back into my eyes. Then I replied to the email and started stretching.

Even with three bras, big boobs will always feel like they are going to tear off your body when you run. This is just physics. But that day, when they bounced and ached and tugged, I felt a newfound hope. I swallowed the pain down and ran faster. Do it, I taunted them silently. I fucking dare you.

*

As a teenager everyone seemed to think my massive honking boobs were awesome except for me. One night, I went with my mother to a yoga class taught by her Witch friend Camille. Afterward, as I rolled up my mat, Camille felt inclined to come over and offer some womanly advice.

A lot of girls are insecure and slouch their shoulders because they have small boobs, she explained. But you don't! So, you should be—and here she stretched her shoulders back wide, thrusting her chest forward in a demonstration of how proudly buxom I could be if only I improved my posture. I smiled thinly and thanked her.

Once, I went to the beach with a friend I hadn't seen in years. When I took my shirt off, she was delighted by my full bikini top. Woah! she said. Where did those come from!? I wish I had boobs like that.

No, you don't, I said immediately.

Why? she asked, but I couldn't think of a reason that wasn't depressing, that didn't bring up back pain or underboob sweat, so I just shrugged. Lucky for me, my shoulders were always in a position ready to shrug.

You've got great boobs, my friend tried to reassure me again, later, when I came out of the water and immediately wrapped a towel around my chest. Flaunt it, girl!

But I was decidedly unable to flaunt it, girl. I was being told from every angle that big boobs are the shit: men love them, women covet them, and if you have them you are very lucky and should know instinctively how to present them in a way that optimizes their appeal. But I just couldn't. I didn't know what was wrong. Somehow, my big boobs seemed like the only two glaring exceptions to the big boob rule. When people spoke about the fun of big boobs, they didn't seem to mean mine. They didn't mean boobs in the shape of tube socks with two tennis balls at the bottom. They didn't mean boobs that seemed to take up more than half your body.

Or maybe they did. Maybe my boobs did do it for some people but I was just so unnecessarily and cripplingly insecure that it was ruining everyone's fantasy. Maybe my boobs were a gifted pair of exceptionally talented racehorses, and I was simply ill-equipped to train them to their full potential. Either way, what I got out of all these interactions was this: my boobs were not the problem. The problem was that they were attached to me.

*

They send me home from my surgery with too-strong painkillers. They make me feel high but not in a fun way, like everything is happening all around me but I'm not privy to any of it. But I need them so that the gnawing in my chest doesn't become a snapping bite, so I gag them down with dry water. I don't feel hunger. I wonder, off-handedly, if I might lose weight during the recovery time, and this thought is calming. Already getting started on a new body to match my new boobs.

It is very hard to sleep. I usually sleep on my side, but I cannot do this, so I'm forced to stay sluggish on my back, staring at the ceiling. My brain doesn't trust me to go fully unconscious again after what happened last time. But it feels fun, giddy, that first night; I feel like a child up past midnight on New Year's. I watch Animal Planet on mute in an attempt to tire my eyes. My chest shrieks dully, bandages constricting my breasts like birds in a tight-fisted cage. I absentmindedly hover my hands above them, palms domed. Soothing. Hush, we'll get through this together. Hush now. Imagine, me and my body finally on the same side. On screen a snake gargles an egg through its body, and we stay smiling.

*

Even though I'd been with my girlfriend for several months by the time I was seventeen, I was still mortified for her to see my boobs. She knew they were big, obviously, but I'd done a pretty good job of hiding just *how* big. We'd only ever made out in dark tents and borrowed bedrooms, and if it were up to me we could have gone on like that for years, my body forever dim and horizontal. But now I was kneeling in front of her in a sports bra at 3pm in my childhood room, everything going numb, my breath heavy and thick.

You okay? she asked gently. She was already shirtless and perfect. I felt the need to warn her.

Yeah, I said, laughing sadly. I just really hate my boobs.

The daylight illuminated her nodding, understanding face. I really wished we weren't doing this in daylight.

When I peeled my bra off, I felt them fall heavy like lifeless offerings to a table. I didn't dare look down. She made no noise, but bent and started to kiss me. It was nice. It was so nice, but I didn't feel a fucking thing. I kept my eyes closed until we were back under the covers, until the light in my room shifted from beige to blue to black. What I can't see won't hurt me. At the very least, it will hurt a lot less.

*

When I return home with my bandages off, my mother insists she do her energy work on me. Energy work is a lot like praying, because you hold your hands a certain way, and it only seems to work if you want it to. She hovers her hands an inch above my freshly hacked breasts, saying Yeah, I feel the heat there. I lie still, eyes closed. When I was younger, this was how she soothed me: not with touch but with the proximity of it.

She returns home the next day with little crystals that she bought from a woman named Karen who sells essential oils and spices and overpriced little crystals. There's a white crystal for healing, jade for protection, amethyst because it's our birthstone, though she cites another reason. I thank her and lay them in the valley of my chest, hoping at least part of me wants them to work. After a while, they just feel cold so I take them off.

I feel tired and ravenous for days, though I eat little. I mostly sleep. When I muster up the energy, I stumble into the bathroom and just stare at my tits like a gross ogling man or a sweet hungry baby. I turn myself this way and that, running a hand gently over the diminished bumps again and again. I can't help it. I can't stop staring. I can't stop thinking, Okay. Okay. So this is what my body is meant to look like.

*

My bruises have soured into a lovely piss-yellow that almost resembles skin. Five days post-op, and I'm poking my boobs every hour now, like fruit waiting to ripen. Slight touch still nauseates, but I am soft, holding them as I would a breath. Fingers poised as if to puncture.

They're still hard like silicon, like implants. The idea of someone mistaking my surgery for an augmentation is delightful to me. I conduct the confrontation in my head: *those things real?* sneers an imaginary man. No, fake, I tell him proudly. Chest out, lip pout. They certainly feel fake. I keep having to remind myself that nothing has been added to me, only taken away. My body does not yet feel like my own, and so it is much easier to love.

I've had a lot of surgeries in my life, but this one is by far the sexiest. I feel stupid and seductive. I feel like the painkillers must still be in my system. I feel like a snake, like Eve, like something too good to be true, too good to be. All I know is I'm bloodied and bruised and take four antibiotics a day, and my scars seep blood and puss, but I feel way too good to care. All I know is that before, I'd never compare my body to any food people would actually eat. All I know is that before, my breasts pulled my shoulder blades down, but now I'd throw open any overcoat with ease. I'd show anyone. C'mon folks, I'd say. Step right up, step right up, come see the tits on this one. The magical self-deflating balloons, the malleable Frisbee girl, whose body was passed from latex-hand to latex-hand before finally being returned to her, pornographic and perplexing and utterly foreign. Step right up, don't be shy—God knows she isn't. C'mon. Get it while it's hot.

September 2023

Give Me Convenience or Give Me Death

Jillian Luft

It's Friday night. I'm getting fingered in a parked RV in my boyfriend's driveway while Jello Biafra snarls about his cock being big enough to make him a star. My boyfriend is a skateboarder. His friends are skateboarders. My younger brother is a skateboarder, too. They're all here now—distant but rowdy silhouettes drinking OE800s, cracking jokes.

I'm not a skateboarder. I'm just a girl in ghost white Adidas and knock-off Vamp lipstick who loves boys with piercings and peroxide hair. My boyfriend has both. Soon, he'll be inked from neck to shin. Soon, he'll buy a used Toyota Corolla and trick it out with rims, a sickass spoiler, and yellow racing stripes. He loves The Descendents, the New York Yankees, and pro skater, Mike Maldonado. Eventually, he'll love me too.

The RV's lights remain off, so my boyfriend's mom won't suspect mayhem. The slightest disturbance (a shattered bottle, that asshole Eric aping Crass and bellowing "I don't give a toss!" for the hundredth time, the bass rumbling out of our janky boombox) and she dashes outside to glower, hands on her hips, her head a dumpling-shaped shadow clouding up the camper's windshield. But she's so overworked, she doesn't really give a shit. It's just for show. My skater boyfriend routinely clambers out and assures her we're all leaving soon. So soon, he lies, until she trudges back indoors to her TV programs and secret cigarettes.

The RV is dank and trashed. The younger kids share joints. The older ones drink cheap beer, smoke Newports. My skater boyfriend is straight edge although not super militant. He drinks soda, likes sex. I've already stopped drinking and never smoked. Soon, I'll give up meat for a steady diet of 7-layer burritos and frozen MorningStar Farms faux meat crumbles. Pretty soon, I'll lose my virginity.

Soon, my skater boyfriend will tattoo "poison-free" onto his tanned forearm in Old English font, the Chinese symbol for "vegetarian" on the tender underside of his wrist. But at this moment, his naked arm is obscured by a glow-in-the-dark cast. He broke his wrist mid-heelflip or truck stand, or while trying one of the other million unearthly tricks in those skate videos we watch repeatedly. He brags about pins in his wrist, complains about the odor.

My skater boyfriend buries his good hand in my baby blue corduroys and aimlessly plunges. He's so damn pretty his ineptitude's almost endearing. Sometimes I wish we went out on real dates, but we've only been going out a couple months. Plenty of time to get to the mall movie theater, the Applebee's nearby. Besides, we hang out almost every day.

Weekdays after school, the skate crew descends upon drugstore parking lots, filling the asphalt with the oceanic roar of their wheels long past dark. Inevitably, the pigs arrive with their empty threats and trespassing warrants. We receive our slips with a smirk because we know we'll be back. No one gets arrested here except for dope dealers and our dads when they drive home drunk from the Ale House.

Our favorite drugstore is the Eckerd's where we use our five-finger discount on boxed hair dye, slathering our strands in their customer restroom, stuffing the pockets of our baggy khakis with Airheads, forking over loose change for those giant rainbow-whirled lollipops that remind us of childhood.

Us girls squat in front of the automatic doors, sucking on our fructose spirals, our scalps fizzing with transformation. The boys fly and flutter above the asphalt. Hardcore butterflies grinding against curbs, suspending themselves in the no-see-um breeze. Shirts lifted, feet tethered. They cheer on every attempt at a kickflip or fakie or whatever the hell. To them, it's all love and physics and temporary freedom from this shithole town, this shithole life. But I remain an object at rest desperate for her unbalanced force.

When I'm not here, I'm a girl splayed across her bed writing bad poetry. Indolent with longing. When the devil compels me, I exercise in manic bursts to Nine Inch Nails' *Pretty Hate Machine.* I wish the devil compelled me more often. And not just to exercise. I'm afraid I'm wasting the best years of my life. I'm afraid nothing will come along and let me transcend myself, whether through pleasure or pain or both—like all my favorite songs promise.

In the secluded back of the RV, I lie supine and sober except for the intermittent pulse of dopamine when my skater boyfriend stumbles upon my clit. My friend Winnie is sprawled out next to me, raving about The Cure's "The Lovecats." I'm kinda annoyed that Winnie's only now discovering *Staring at the Sea,* essentially a greatest hits album. But whatever. I mutter feeble "uh huhs" while my skater boyfriend kisses my neck, his fingers still digging their way inside of me. A raw but mild ache. Like yanking out a dry tampon.

I find my skater boyfriend's tongue again, lean into the dependable crook of his fiberglass arm. That asshole Eric rewinds side 2 so The Dead Kennedys can repeat their tired rebellion. Soon, these lame-ass parties will end, and our crew of scrubs and gutter punks and working-class weirdos will slowly disband. My boyfriend will drive us to the mall movie theater, to Applebee's, to work at the supermarket that also employs his mom.

Soon, we'll fall in love and swear it's forever. So soon. But not just yet. Tonight, our wheels remain stationary. Tonight, it's the tepid glow of his hand through the black and the yeasty, Frito's smell of boys and our clothed bodies attempting new tricks, cheering each other on. Tonight, there's time for my skater boyfriend to push himself against me and propel me somewhere outside of myself. Somewhere I can't find. Somewhere better and new. There's still so much time for us to do nothing. My dad won't pick me up for hours.

October 2021

VIOLENCE

The Knife on the Necklace

Lyd Havens

I found it in a basement consignment store downtown on the last day of May, while thunder knocked against the sky. The knife is silver, folded into the body of a brass fish, hooked into a metal circle, and fits perfectly in my palm.

I wear the knife around my neck, on the same chain as the golden hawk pendant my grandparents gave me when I was in high school. That summer, I had seen a medium in New Jersey. She told me my late uncle watched over me through hawks. Driving away from her office, a hawk was perched on every telephone line.

The knife is heavier than the hawk pendant, but its weight comforts me.

To unfold, I fit my thumbnail into the curve of the handle and draw it back like I'm opening a door. The blade isn't sharp, but it's still a utility. I use it to open packages or cut stray strings away from my shirts. Once, my roommate and I were walking through a parking garage when a girl stopped us to ask if we could help her stagnant car. We used the knife to cut a plastic water bottle into a funnel to feed oil into her engine. When I re-clasped the necklace, a petal-shaped oil stain bloomed against my sternum.

I had always wanted a knife of my own. As a child, I secretly admired my father's pocketknife, with its double blades and faux mother-of-pearl casing. He found it on the floor of the downtown bar he cleaned for a living, or next to the dumpster around the back. Perhaps one of his friends that always asked to crash on our couch gave it to him as some token of gratitude.

As I grew taller, leaner, supposedly more appealing, he began to lend me the pocketknife whenever I walked up our dirt road to get the mail, or to the Minit Market to get an ice cream bar. He would tell me to have both of the blades already unfolded and protruding from my fist as I walked. “If a man ever tries to take you,” he’d repeat, “stab him quick, and not just once.”

Years later, he asked me why I was so afraid of men.

Wearing a knife around my neck, no matter how small and dull, sends the message that I am on high alert, or prepared for violence. I am neither—even after growing up in violence, nobody can ever be truly prepared—and yet I wear the knife all the same. I don’t have to use it; I just have to touch it. To have it resting right next to the hawk, symbolizing the first great loss of my life, feels like resilience: Here is what I have lost, and here is the security I have made for myself from its aftermath.

September 2021

Big and Little

Christy Tending

I would never actually hit you, he told me. As if it were obvious. As if that was the line. I sat on the counter staring at him. I had recoiled when he punched the cabinet, feeling the wind of his fist in my ear. I'm not sure, in retrospect, if I was challenging him, or simply too shocked to speak or look anywhere else. I looked into his face, searching for a shred of what wasn't there. He looked into my face in return, registering my fear, becoming angrier. Furious I had responded to this outburst. His embarrassment only fed his rage. *I would never actually hit you.*

In my life, there has been big violence and little violence. The big violence is, strangely, easier to talk about: the big, showy, state-sponsored violence is easy to see. Look, there is the tear gas, here are the flash-bangs.

I can demonstrate it: my right shoulder still doesn't move properly after a cop dislocated it. I can remember the dirt road in Canada where it happened, I can explain what it's like to be surveilled by helicopters for days on end at a logging blockade. Somehow, the violence and the invasive violation of having my phone tapped sparks a bigger reaction. The big violence—of having loved ones arrested and jailed, of the weight of a found rubber bullet in my hand, of telling my body not to run when that's all it wants to do—this is easier to explain. The way I've been handcuffed and left in the back of a van with no air conditioning, please understand.

The little violence looked like this: *I would never actually hit you.* (Although, his fist had just connected with the cupboard a few inches from my face, so forgive my confusion.) And the violence looked like his dead expression when he learned he was the one who made me recoil in fear. The little violence sounds like, *What's the big deal?*

The way I became smaller and smaller, until I could fit in the palm of your hand. Until I was sweet, pocket-sized.

If it was real, I was supposed to have a black eye, to have something to show for it. To be real, it needed to be big. I was supposed to have earned this pain. That would make it glorious and believable. Instead, the violence was so small from the outside, it was almost microscopic. You needed to get close to see it, which is why by the end, I barely had any friends besides the truly persistent. If he let me have friends, it stood to reason, they would get close enough to see the truth. His friends were my friends, he argued. And I didn't argue back.

One day, lying on his bed, I was reading *Ecology Against Capitalism*—I will never forget this; my dog-eared copy is still on my bookcase after sixteen years. He asked me what I was reading, and I showed him the book. He asked what it was about, and I read him a recently highlighted bit. *For school or for fun?* It was a little bit of both.

You shouldn't do that, he said. *It makes me feel stupid, like I'm not at smart as you.* As he'd promised, he did not hit me, but stalked out of the room, enraged. I heard him banging around in the kitchen a few seconds later. This is little violence, of course: a tiny, but cruel act of trying to make me smaller and less bright. It took years to convince me this would have been enough to leave him right then. This is the trouble with little violence: it takes so much more convincing it is wrong.

His words picked at my skin until I was invisibly bloodied. Sometimes, I could laugh them off. See? I could say with my fake face, *I am unbothered. I can love your cruelty, which means, perhaps, I am also loveable?* The question mark, hanging in the air, hoping he would swoop it out of the way and say he was kidding. (Which, it should seem plainly obvious, never happened.)

This was little violence: no flash-bangs or pepper spray or nights in jail. This little violence looked like fury when I didn't answer my phone. It felt like being accused of sleeping with my friends until I could count them on one hand. It was the slow wearing-down of a person who is ignored and treated as disposable, until she is needed for something specific, in which case she is expected to be present and cheerful.

It's not like I ever hit you, he says when I tell him I'm unhappy.

It is little violence, as though that's true—as though that matters. *It is little violence,* still trying to convince myself all these years later. But it is not. It is no small thing, this erosion of self. It is little-ing: making me smaller and smaller. It is not little, but belittling.

And what about my own violence? The way I abandoned myself on the side of the road in the middle of the night. The way I let my small, young self believe she deserved it. I gave up on the unwieldy parts of myself, left those to the junkyard dogs to fight over.

The little violence is insidious because it makes me wonder whether it happened at all. Or whether I was making it up. Maybe I took it the wrong way. Maybe he didn't mean it. It makes me wonder whether I am as crazy as he told me I was. It makes me question where the line is, whether it was violence, whether I had the right to be afraid of him and make him feel bad.

It was small enough to keep me close because I knew how good it would feel when it would stop; small enough that stopping felt possible. One day, I thought. I will be good enough not to bring this on myself. I didn't leave him because of any of this, amazingly enough.

March 2023

The Taste and Shape of Survival

Lena Ziegler

On a trip across state lines, I rent a room safer than any home, devoid of any identity. A man has been texting me. He knows what hotel I'll be staying at. He knows the velvet of my inner thighs. He knows I'm only staying for the night. I'm sure he has a name.

When he arrives, he texts, *I'm here.*

I wait for his knock, to be greeted by the barrel of him. I stare at the hotel's fire escape instructions posted beneath the peephole. My lips are sticky and my tongue is dry. I contemplate all the uses for a human mouth. I contemplate the journey between survival and burning.

In the many years I've introduced my body to strange men, I've never lost sight of the danger. How, if they wanted to, they could lay me down, slice me open, and bleed me out, before slipping away unscathed and satisfied, as my heart pumps swells of black cherry insides into the bedsheets, soaking through to the mattress pad, imbuing the air with inside-out-human scent. This fear pummels me in the moments before their arrival, when nervous energy radiates, and I question my reasons for everything. But on rainwater nights, alone with my ache for relevance and escape, it's easy to believe the intentions of strange men, however brutal, cannot be worse than those of the men I have already known. Such thoughts can be comforting, in the way a gunshot to the head might appeal to anyone suffering a long, slow death. Even with their bodies hovering above mine, faces twisting to cum, sweat dripping brow to lip, an animal exchange of currency, I've never stopped picturing it happening long enough to believe that a man might choose not to destroy a woman, if given the opportunity. If given a proper opening. Though I've never been proven right, in time I've come to reason that to a womanbody, so many times broken, there may be a greater danger in believing he won't. That the illusion of safety from any man, at any point in time, might ripen more than my body for the inevitability of violence.

These are the thoughts I run from.

I open the door, and he steps inside with his shoulder-length hair tied back half way, like me at twelve, ignored at a middle school dance.

You look pretty, he says.

Thanks.

He is taller than expected, face thinner and longer. Cigarette-breath stale with habit.

So you're just visiting for the night? he asks, and I hate his voice. I don't remember his name.

Let's not talk.

I smile when I say it, so it isn't rude, but I know it doesn't matter if it is or isn't, because he's on the bed, balancing on bony knees above me.

Fifteen minutes later, and I am not dead yet.

He is licking my body and my throat is feeling to moan and my muscles are feeling to clench, but I know this won't happen because my body is numb to his. In all his licking, I wait for the familiar burn to rise from my stomach, to my nipples, to my throat, for the sheets to singe beneath us, the curtains to catch, and the room to glow unbridled, flame charring everything with the sear of want satisfied.

But when we touch, there is nothing.

His fingers are in my hair, nose pressed against my neck, and I am safe floating somewhere above us. I can no longer taste his cigarette. I cannot hear his voice.

He pushes himself inside of me, and I am thinking about his mother. A woman who gave life to a man, *this* man, and somehow went on living. I consider the risk in giving your body to someone, spreading it open and spewing life from your depths. Letting go and bouncing back. Surrendering without retreating. There is more than one way to use a body.

I've seen men do magic.

I've seen my silhouette in mirrors.

I've been frayed and split and spit into oblivion.

I've seen legs clamp shut, mouth lockjaw, gaping unguarded.

I've seen women bend back humanity like a whisper in their hands.
I've been war torn and ugly with nowhere to run.

My back is flat against the ceiling, a mirror of myself below, all plastered and unmoving. Nowhere to run. On the bed, I am stillness, lonely in the atrophy of body crumbling beneath shoulder-length hair like a middle-school dance: not belonging anywhere, waiting to be wanted, learning to breathe underwater. I have gone hollow in the eyes, and I wonder if he's noticed that in a different life I could have been anything else but this open sore, undressing my wounds before him, like dying in reverse.

In the many years I've been myself, I've contemplated the taste and shape of survival. The many uses of a human mouth. How a whisper and a scream can sound exactly the same given the right temperature. It's been months since the Last Man and I haven't craved sex, just filling. There is no escape from this body, with both its magic and tragedy bearing the truth of so much male memory. If I could count my pulse like rings in a tree, I might discover there's no one left.

Suddenly he pulls out of me and stands up at the end of the bed.

I am back in my body.

Shifting to my knees, my gaze clings to his tiny mouth, all twisted in disgust. I ask what he wants to do next, but he pulls on his jeans. I don't understand. Then I see it, just below me.

I have spilled onto the sheets a giant pool of black cherry insides.

He is pulling a sweater over his hairless chest.

I have bled through to the mattress pad.

I am apologizing.

He shrugs.

It happens, he says, like periods happen, like everything has an ending.

My fingertips graze the sticky warmth of menstrual blood, one-week early, human-sized, whale-sized, galaxy-wide and forever expanding, the blood of my womanbody soaking opaque like a middle school dance: crying in a bathroom, zip-up hoodie tied around my waist, veiling my lineage of so much ripping.

Sixteen years post-puberty and I am still ashamed and asking forgiveness. He asks when I'll be back in the city, and I lie *never* again.

The door clicks shut behind him and I am alone.

For a while I cry. My throat closes in on itself and I can hardly breathe through the humiliation I feel, the utter, impenetrable aloneness, galaxy-wide and forever expanding. I order room service and eat it with my fingers, right next to the bloodstain I made but didn't die for. In the background SVU: the violence of too many malebodies and not enough justice, but in the years to come I will know my many survivals better than the sound of my own voice screaming. I will know myself as more than an object, war-torn with nowhere to run. Years from now, I will know myself.

I chew my food and I begin to laugh.

I wonder about the dried stain of my insides left behind on his dick, how it will feel when he stands in the shower and the pinkish lather of soap blossoms in his hand, a reminder of me.

I wonder about the shape my blood takes in the grooves of his fingertips, and I am certain that before me he has never known the blood of a womanbody pooled neatly beneath him, all Rorschach without apology.

I wonder if the iron taste of me still lingers in his mouth, if I am a memory he can't escape, and if I, with my blood, am his version of violence.

I wonder if this is the last time I will introduce my body to a strange man in a hotel room, but I won't be certain of that for a few more years, when I learn to love my body for all it can be when it's no longer an object to be split open by unrelenting men.

I am certain this isn't the last time he will introduce his body to a strange woman in a hotel room.

I am certain that if I hadn't bled through to the mattress pad, if he hadn't pulled back in disgust and slipped gently into the night, that I would have stayed there for however long it took until it was over, thinking about his mother, the many uses for a human mouth, and the curious art of surrendering without retreating, without saying a word.

And I am certain he wouldn't have noticed.

July 2021

Shutter Speed

Cameron Gearen

There's a series of photos in which I'm posing with my biological father on the small front porch of his townhome in Anchorage, Alaska. It's summertime, 1983, and brilliant outside until nearly midnight this far north. A potted hanging fuchsia on the edge of the photo frame spills copious blossoms, riotous.

My dad and I are both dressed up. It is the summer before he dies, but he hasn't been diagnosed yet. In these photos, he looks well, with ruddy cheeks and shiny eyes. The oozing melanoma behind his ear, the one that is leaking all over every pillowcase he owns and that he's refusing to get checked, may have already metastasized to his lungs. In any case, his body is a time bomb and he's doing nothing about it, and that decision will cost him his life in nine short months, when he dies on April 8, 1984.

But I'm getting ahead of myself.

*

In the series of photos, I'm wearing a teal cotton dress I borrowed from his girlfriend (who will become, briefly, my stepmother in the middle of the winter, marrying my by-then emaciated chemo patient father in someone's sunken living room). I am wearing a white headband and my hair is cut in a bob, with bangs. I have just turned fourteen.

If you look at the photos—as my mother did when I got home to Chicago later that month—you might see something amiss, something almost too subtle to name. It might give you a prickly feeling on the back of your neck. My father and I are posed in the frame, over and over, with a positioning reserved for lovers. I am inclining my head toward his as one does to a boyfriend or husband, never to a parent. I am fingering the button on his dinner jacket the way adult women flirt with their spouses or lovers. I am playing the coquette. He is playing the gallant.

When my mother saw these pictures, she waited one day, asked me to show them to her again, and then asked me if my father had ever harmed me. I assured her (and my own unquiet brain) that he had not. She had asked me that once before, shortly after they divorced when I was three and my father gained sole weekend access to me. When I came home crying and making my stuffed mouse, Algernon, aggressively kiss my Raggedy Ann doll, she was worried. I denied it then too. She looked for marks on my small body at bath time but found none.

I learned much later that my father had been sexually violent to my mother. She also told me much later that she never imagined he would do to me what he had done to her.

But I'm getting ahead of myself.

*

When I told her he had not harmed me, I was telling the truth as I knew it, based on what was available within my conscious mind. The actual truth of the ways he did harm me would remain sealed away in my unconscious mind for twenty-five years from that day in my 1983 kitchen. In fact, my father's untimely death may have sent my memories back into the crypt for some extra decades as I worked overtime to "grieve" my father. Dramatically pining for him covered up the real story: that he groomed me to be his child lover, that he violently raped me dozens of times. My mother, who loved and loves me fiercely, experienced her neck prickling as she looked at those photos. Even she was helpless in the face of my denial, a force that made my own story unavailable to myself.

How does one learn to pose as a sexualized grown woman by age thirteen, reminiscent of a blue movie before one has ever seen one? How does one wear the vestments of adult sexuality convincingly?

*

When my daughters were little, they loved to pilfer my lipstick and draw bright, clownish lips around their own. They wrapped themselves in my shawls, found mismatched pairs of my heels, slipped their small feet in, and clomped around our apartment. They were little girls trying on my shoes and mannerisms, not pulling it off by any stretch—looking more like a zany circus act than like their adult mother.

When I was their age, I had been someone's unwilling lover for years already. One year at Baptist summer camp, nestled in the remote Davis Mountains in southern Texas, I suggested my cabinmates and I, for our final skit on parents' night, devise a dance set to Donna Summers' "Bad Girls," a 1979 hit about prostitutes. Somehow, my idea was greenlit, and I threw myself into choreographing. Although my counselor fixed my hair in chaste French braids, I could "work it" better than anyone else, throwing my hips with a prescience that, if it hadn't been the checked-out, groovy seventies, might have caused a well-meaning adult some alarm. For an otherwise sheltered child who rarely was allowed to watch network TV, some internal instinct—that of being an adult, sexual woman—had been awoken far before its time; I came by my sluttiness naturally as I had been taught the Lolita role by a master Humbert Humbert. Like those movies about A+ students who turn tricks on the weekend, I led a double life. The remarkable thing is that my double life was a secret to myself.

*

I had my first flashback on a rainy April night in 2008. It was triggered by the panicked voice of my older—very shy—daughter who was trying to be brave by toughing it out at a sleepover, but who called me from the tiled bathroom at her friend's house. I can still hear her tiny, terrified voice traveling through the family's portable phone into my landline. I offered to pick her up, and she whispered that, no, she wanted to stay. When I hung up the phone, my brain exploded in what I can only describe as a sepia-toned "movie" with frames of things I didn't recognize but later (and with a torrent of new flashbacks) was able to stitch together into a story—one of terrible abuse and violence that stretched from the time I was three (when my parents divorced) to the year I was fourteen (when my biological father died).

At the time, I was working in therapy with a skilled and experienced clinician. I had started with N three years earlier, complaining that I lived inside a cloud of self-loathing. Over the years, N had asked me to tell her more about my relationship with my biological dad. I always answered, "There's nothing more to tell. I loved him, and he died young," and she nodded as we moved to the next topic. I don't know if N's skin prickled when I dismissed her questions, if she had some sense there was more to the story. If so, she never betrayed her worries or got out ahead of me.

The morning after my first flashback, I called N. I said, "It's not me. It's incest."

*

To survive within my hellish reality as a child, I had to code switch between little girl and vixen. I hate to think what would have happened to me at the hands of my father had I not played both parts very well. Who was taking those pictures, as I stood with my father on the porch that afternoon? My future stepmother was there—maybe blind to any prickling of her own neck, as she had been incested by her own father (she had told me). My aunt was also there, my father's only sister, someone who lionized the version of my father that was visible to the world—Yale law degree, basketball star, piano prodigy, handsome hipster. Something canceled out any neck-prickling she might have had, had she considered the strangely comely angle of my neck that day. Many years later, she conceded he was a sociopath. But I'm getting ahead of myself.

My mind couldn't know about my abuse, but eventually my body did. It showed me movie-like tapes that unfurled in my mind's eye with alarming steadiness, often viewed from the point of view of the top of the doorframe. In my thirties, as in my teens, I was relatively sheltered; I read Jane Austen for pleasure and had never seen video porn. If they weren't memories, where could these vivid scenes have come from, replete with specific and long "forgotten" details of the many houses and apartments where my dad had lived? I wanted to believe they were an illusion or fiction, but I couldn't deny their realness. Consider the scene in which I'm maybe five years old, taking a bath in a rented farmhouse while my dad cooks dinner in the kitchen with whichever girlfriend he has invited on this weekend (she is out of the frame of my recovered memory). I take the bar of soap and wash my vulva, which produces a pain so sharp it blinds me. I scream and scream, and my dad comes running, yelling at me for making a scene. He tells me not to wash down there anymore. In my mind's eye, he is vivid—the cadence of his voice, his jeans studded with rhinestones and fringed with burrs from our walk to the pond earlier that day. As I watch this internal movie now as an adult, I realize my tissues must have been torn, and putting soap on an open cut caused the split of white-hot pain.

*

Besides the internal "photography," there are many actual photographs. My father dabbled and left behind binders of prints and negatives: me in leotards, photographed from odd and suggestive angles, standing in a field of marram grass, like an X-rated baby Helga. I saved everything through many moves and left myself a breadcrumb trail. Then I walked the trail and reconstructed my life. I have sifted through it all, including a postcard he sent me from Las Vegas when I was eight (says the postmark); on the front of the card is a photograph of a neon sign—the iconic woman sitting inside an oversized martini glass, her sexy gams thrown over its lip. On the back, my father wrote to my eight-year-old self, "I didn't expect to find you here!" Maybe a funny joke—comparing your child to a neon lady of the night—but only funny if it's preposterous. Not funny if it's merely true.

The shards and scenes now live in my conscious mind. Occasionally

I hear it can't be true—that "memory doesn't work like that." My father's sister shared this opinion. I am here to tell you that traumatic memory works exactly like that. From the other women in my trauma group to those whose stories populate books like *The Body Keeps the Score* and *Trauma and Recovery,* we all hope you understand that traumatic memory—preserved in amber for later consideration—does indeed work just like this.

*

It has been fourteen years since that chilly April night when I first had a glimmer of my abuse history. Facing it has been the hardest work of my life so far. When I did the work to stitch the memories together, everything "clicked." This hidden narrative was the mystery dictating all my choices; it explains why I have to leave a store if I hear 1970's funk, why I must excuse myself from the company of men with mustaches, why I avoid ranch-style homes, why I never wanted to have biological kids of my own and instead chose to adopt in my twenties, why I became a poet. I lost my aunt because she disagrees, my first marriage because who really can with all that, and the comfortable haze of denial I used to live inside, but, by allowing the truth in, I gained my very self. I forgot to remember, and then I remembered to live.

June 2022

About Accidental Firearm Discharge on Campus

Paul Rousseau

After my best friend shot me in the head through two walls in our on-campus apartment by freak accident, every news outlet in the Twin Cities threw something together for quick clicks. Reading them felt dirty to me. Like a bad sex joke etched into the bathroom stall at a Kum N' Go.

Most of the information was just plain wrong. Crucial context was laughably withheld. Other pieces altogether false. Imagine watching the NBA finals, but every article the next day is littered with wild inconsistencies. Stats are skewed. Plays invented. The other team won when yours actually did. That's what it felt like when I read these articles. Guesses and approximations were thrown together and delivered with a staggering conviction of truth. As if two totally separate events existed in the same parcel of time and space.

Every article covered the basics. This University. That police department. Here were the times, roughly. The students are both male, twenty-two years old, one from this city, the other from that city. Some included my name. None included my best friend's. The articles assured us that it was not an act of violence, which is debatable. They stressed it was an accident, he was just fooling around with a gun, then, oops, pulled the trigger, which doesn't necessarily mean it wasn't violent. It was a very violent accident. Those things are not mutually exclusive. We were assured the weapon, never *weapons*, no one knows about the plural weapons he hid away in the trunk of his car after he shot me—we were assured that the guilty weapon was taken into police custody and that there was no current threat beyond that.

We were assured that the twenty-two year old suspect (news sources don't typically name suspects before they are charged or arrested) was no longer on campus, which was untrue. We were told with confidence that no one was likely to bump into him by chance. Wrong again, my girlfriend did just days later, overwhelmed and appalled, already overwhelmed and appalled from the incident, then doubly so after running into him. The police confirmed that he had a valid permit to carry when his gun accidentally went off. Our concern is directed again and again to his permit to carry. This, for them, is the salient detail. As if it were to make the whole situation a little less horrific, and somewhat ok.

Some articles wanted us to know that the bullet was fired through a wall. Or possibly two walls, then into the common area. Some articles wanted us to know that the suspect at the time was not visible to the other student who was shot, that is, me. Most articles wanted us to know that the student, me again, was transported to the hospital. None of the articles devoted word count to the severity of the injury, the critical care and subsequent surgery, or, of course, the slurry of bizarre circumstances leading up to said emergency admittance. Namely my best friend's refusal to get help for two nightmarish hours while he prioritized his own fate before mine. Faced with the fear of going to jail and scrubbing toilets for the rest of his life, he insisted we go to Home Depot for paint and quick-dry plaster to repair the bullet holes in the wall, less concerned with the one on my head. All while blood from a source eerily close to my brain soaked through the bottom of a pillowcase. It wasn't until my other roommate came home from volleyball practice that he was convinced, outnumbered, to call 911.

A gun went off, went through some walls, then made contact with another human. At the time, that's really all that's known for certain. What word would best fit that scenario? A student was hit? Struck? Injured? All serviceable, though "shot" is probably the safest bet. Those words were not used. Instead, the word *grazed* was deployed, almost ubiquitously, in every article. The meaning of *grazed*, according to whichever dictionary Google prioritizes, "to scrape the skin, or a part of the body, so as to break the surface but cause little or no bleeding."

Ah, yes. Grazed. The bullet touched the gentleman's head lightly in passing, shattering a portion of his skull bone before ricocheting off onto the carpet. Only a healthy trail of blood smatter, some alarming red handprints on the wall, were found leading to the bathroom mirror. The abrasion merely caused severe brain trauma, a scratch really, along with reconstructive neurosurgery that resulted in the addition of a few titanium plates and screws implanted in the head. Being a scuff, quite minor, the gentleman will struggle through a life of various physical and psychological residual symptoms, requiring numerous therapies, medications, specialty appointments, that is, complaints to be taken lightly given the stark horror of the insignificant nick.

Some articles mentioned that I'm an English major.

March 2023

How Pretty the Trigger Sits Idle in the Weapon

Erin Slaughter

This summer, while I was sweating in a Wisconsin dorm room and chewing watermelon-flavored Double Bubble, masturbating to fantasies of J not noticing my fifteen-pound weight gain at the hands of the camp cafeteria's pasta bar, my mom texted me: *S died. I just found out, cancer.* The ellipsis bubble hovered on my phone screen. *He was my first...you know what I mean?* The man my mother began dating the day she, my sister and I moved to Texas after her divorce from my father, a man who shared the same name as my father, who lived with us (as all her boyfriends lived with us) in tenseness punctuated by blow-out shouting matches for a little over a year—my mom's once-high school sweetheart—was dead. Rather than the last words he left her with, a slimy-drunken voicemail on our home phone threatening to kill himself, the fact that she had lost her virginity to him won out in her memory. That he was someone she had loved, before she didn't. *The two S's in my life, both lost now,* she wrote.

When I consider my mother's relationship to men—my father, S, a string of others, and my now-stepdad—I believe her to be the subject of a kind of violence, though she would never describe herself that way. Though I've never known her to be hit by any of them, I remember how she worked twelve hours a day and came home as if tip-toeing over nails to wash my stepdad's oil-stained jeans, cook some kind of dinner he would eat, and would often end up out in the garage getting yelled at anyway. I remember how my stepdad never hit her, but he threw a knife at the wall so hard it got stuck in the cheap plaster, how he cornered us against the stairs, red-faced and screaming, and dented our front door, just over my mother's shoulder, when he threw a baby bottle in her direction as she stood holding my infant sister. Now that I am older, I feel sorry for my mother. I have tried to become the opposite of her, but to be any kind of woman is to be violence-adjacent, no matter where you live or what job or degrees you have or whether or not you choose to have children.

A few nights ago, I was lying in bed with J and told him, tentatively, politely, that I would prefer he not choke me during sex anymore. It was something I'd asked for when we first started dating, and something he had grown to like, so I felt guilty about taking it away. Guilty about asking for anything to be different than it was. He, of course, agreed completely, but wanted to understand why. I thought about it, and the only word that felt right, even though it didn't feel like mine to use, was *triggered.* I qualified my answer, telling him: *It feels silly to say it that way, though. I mean, nothing has ever* happened *to me.*

I am the only woman I know who has never been raped. In a grotesque way, I add a silent *yet* to that sentence, am always waiting for it to show up like some horrible marker of womanhood, just as we once waited patiently for our turn as our friends descended one by one into the secret cult of menstruation. This struck me for the first time during the Kavanagh hearings, that I had no way to understand the terror and shame coming through my female friends' eyes and social media posts, that I had no #MeToo to add. But also feeling the terror, the shame, that yes, in some way, if not in this specific way, *Me Too.*

When we were together a few weeks ago in Arkansas, I told my best friend, L, about the only time I remember my mom lifting a punishment: I was grounded from going to the seventh-grade school dance, but tearfully told her that my boyfriend would break up with me if I wasn't there, and she immediately told me to get dressed and drove me there. L pointed out the many problems with what this would teach a daughter about men, one of which being: if a boy threatens absence, you come running, no matter what the cost.

L told me once that attention is not the same as kindness, but I have spent more lifetimes than I can count confusing the two, and hoping if they showed up together they would alchemize into love: that prized mirage sealed away for beautiful, thin girls who could pull off middle bangs and had never been so desperate as to consider writing poetry.

For a long time (and maybe even now), though I knew sex was not synonymous with love, it was at least the same as attention. It was the same when, backstage at the high school play, an older boy I'd never spoken to cornered me alone by the dark stairwell and, so close I could smell the gum on his breath, reached into my bra. It was the same when I offered to drive an acquaintance the forty-five minutes home when his car got towed, and he insisted on fingering me, despite my polite and gentle protests, to "thank" me. It was the same when my stepdad's friend, the only adult who I felt had treated me like a full human by listening intently to the story of my eighth-grade heartbreak, got too drunk one night and bent down in the kitchen to demand I let him kiss me, sour breath all over my face. It was the same when only a little over a year ago on that Mississippi porch, I handed N a knife and drunkenly begged him to cut me open.

What counts as a lifetime of violence?

And what if the violence is something we ask for, something we use others as a tool to inflict on ourselves? The last time J choked me during sex, it didn't freak me out because it felt violent, or felt it could lead to violence, but because I realized that I didn't want to have the same kind of destructive sex with him that I'd had with others. Those others, faceless dick-forward blurs inching in a swarm toward my heart like ants toward a smashed cupcake, couldn't hurt me because I never hoped anything of them. But with J, the stakes are real. The trigger already cocked, even if no one's hand has reached for it yet.

Because I spent last week visiting his family for Thanksgiving, and in the sweet moment while watching a movie, when I realized that he and his mom and sister all have the same-shaped toes, and briefly wondered if one day my child will also have those toes, I thought about my mother telling me the story of her first Thanksgiving with my dad's family, and I wondered if she thought some version of the same thing, and all these years later, her S's lost. Because half of the moments I have loved anyone have been curtained with a layer of dread that whoever I choose will end up murdered like my dad, another ghost fed to the machine of the Story. And if that's what it means to be with me, to be threaded into this morose familial karma, shouldn't I save J from it by letting him leave me before he can no longer escape? Because for many years, I believed that to love at all is to hand your body over to be weaponized against you, or to choose to become the weapon.

It is here that I'll admit when I write these essays, I'm usually trying to avoid whatever I'm writing my way around: this week I'm supposed to tackle a major book revision on my memoir, and my agent has asked me to write about gun violence. I don't feel I have that authority, although my dad was killed by a gun in the hand of a person he loved enough to marry, though my mother keeps a loaded handgun in the kitchen island, though each time I walk into a gas station I scan the aisles for the safest place to hide if someone were to walk in and open fire, though each time a news story about another shooting pops up on my phone I rolodex in my mind the names of everyone I love who might live there, of anyone someone I love loves who might live there. I guess the impact of gun violence on my life can be summarized as: I am always trying to avoid letting myself love anything too much.

November 2020

DEATH

FILLED MOUTHS DON'T SLEEP AT NIGHT

Kiyanna Hill

i.

My grandmother and I are dizzy from the sun. She wears a turquoise house dress—the bottom hem moth-eaten and thin. I tell her I'm afraid to sleep. How my bed devours me whole. How my dreams turn thick & black. She doesn't respond, and I repeat myself. I can't move in my sleep, and I swear someone is there to pin me still. Sometimes, I feel hands on my wrists, a hint of sharp tipped nails teasing my pulse.

ii.

We don't attend her funeral. It's hot, and my mother is angry: something something *they took everything* something about disrespect something about thieves & *what about my daughters?* I remember the pink carpet in my bedroom. I remember the sun glaring on my TV. Back then, I obsessed over forensic shows, the discovery of fingerprinting, and cold cases. Somebody was always dead or close to it & there I was soft & sweating with carpet fibers leaving impressions in my thighs. I know I cried with my teeth sunk into a pillow. I thought all grief and agony worked that way, slightly hidden and always ready.

iii.

My grandmother can fall asleep swiftly. After a meal. During the intro to *Days of Our Lives.* Mid-sentence. Mid-story. I had already learned to make myself small & quiet, so I made patterns in the meshed light from the screen door. I was the first thing she looked for when she woke. Always the same question no matter the time of day—*You hungry?* I never said no. There was always food, and unlike my mother, she let me fill myself silly. Root beer floats, Brunswick stew with a spoon of sugar, fried catfish while we watched the stray cats scramble in the yard for scales & insides. This was how I was taught that worry comes later.

vi.

It's witches coming to see you. Mean little things flying at night. We eat on the porch, our fingers slick with grease. I've trained my body to work against sleep. Sounding out words while I read next to my nightlight. Coloring with the blunt ends of crayons. *Does your mama know?* I eat and eat to hold the silence. My grandmother doesn't give me a fix. If the witches only come at a certain time. If I should sleep with my head at the foot of my bed. When she falls asleep, I take her empty plate, throw the bones as far as I can.

October 2022

Dead Express

Danielle Chelosky

In 1854, the London Necropolis Railway started running. It provided the opportunity for grievers to ride with corpses to the Brookwood Cemetery, which was the largest cemetery in the world at the time. In the stations, there were bars with signs that read: "Spirits served here."

*

I became transfixed by Ian Curtis when my ex-boyfriend showed me the film *Control.* I cried toward the end, after the Joy Division singer's suicide. For the whole movie, I felt embarrassed by his stage presence. The jerks and jolts of his body disturbed me. It wasn't even him; it was the actor Sam Riley, but his thick jawline, his empty eyes, and his pitch-black hair made him indistinguishable from Curtis to me. Even after the breakup, my adoration for the enigmatic musician continued. I wanted darkness. There is something profound in utter despair.

*

I imagine sitting alongside passengers on the London Necropolis Railway—which you and I jokingly refer to as the Dead Express—and the sense of unity with other mourners who are looking out the windows, watching the world whirl by us with all of its life while we descend down the bottomlessness of grief.

*

There is a consistent mythologizing and fetishizing of deceased musicians—this much we know, though there is not much to say. I cannot stop participating. I understand just checking it out and moving on, you tell me, like with a car crash, but lately I have been bingeing songs of the dead, even though they are misaligned with my usual taste. It frustrates you, especially when you think the music is bad. You shut down the conversation and say you want to show me something else. *It's almost as morbid as your obsession with dead Soundcloud rappers,* you tell me.

*

When I was little, I would always volunteer to join a parent on a car ride, no matter the destination. I was enamored with the feeling of being in motion; it satiated my curiosity and my need for feeling productive. It temporarily lifted me out of my default state of sadness. Once, I went with my dad on a trip to the bank and slid a CD into the car's slot. I was a teenager then, completely clueless of the fact that a few nights later he would die. *You just wanted to come with me so you could play your music,* he said. The pulsating rock song reverberated through the speakers with a screamed hook: *Die young and save yourself!*

*

Aside from Ian Curtis or dead Soundcloud rappers, I idolize the eccentric artist who was cancelled last year, whose synth-filled songs make me feel as if I am floating through space, untethered and in awe. He rambles ecstatically in interviews to the point of incoherence, and he mimics Curtis' erratic movement on stage. He refers to the latter as practicing "the hysterical body." I am so often embarrassed—embarrassed when I talk, walk, exist. My fear of being perceived worsens each day, feeding into my growing agoraphobia. What would it be like, I wonder, to succumb to the hysterical, to the fullness of feeling? To stand on a pedestal in front of a crowd and close my eyes and jump and whip around my head and limbs?

*

When a man is playing violin in the parking lot, I ask Haley if she ever visits her mom's grave alone when she's home. She says she doesn't. I say I don't visit my dad's either, despite my frequent fantasy of laying in the grass of the cemetery, cocooned in nature, reading a book, watching planes fly away from the private airport across the street. She says she has similar daydreams. But neither of us can bring ourselves to do it. There is something deeply humiliating in the act of admitting grief. It feels cliché, I tell Haley. I don't want to fit into a cliché—to live it out, fall victim to the typical definition of mourning. I want to prove I am something more, even though I am not, because there is nothing to be *more than* in the first place.

*

I imagine myself sitting on the Dead Express, riding back and forth all day, comforted by the constant movement, almost sedated and soothed by the act of existing within a space specifically dedicated for grief. Maybe I would step off to get drunk at the bar—the kind of absurdly wasted that would make people worry about me and friends never talk to me again. What is intoxication if not a way of giving in to our hysterical selves? As soon as I get to your place, I pour myself wine, protected by the excuse of alcohol in case I get too hysterical, too embarrassing.

*

The London Necropolis Railway's last day of service was in 1941. They expected to carry 10,000 to 50,000 bodies per year, but they averaged only 2,300. But grief, I suspect, does not need to be materialized by something as tangible as a train; we can move within our mourning in our own bodies, reckoning and thrashing until we decompose.

July 2022

Bottom of the X

WA Hawkins

I reach for my phone in the morning dark, hate myself briefly for checking it first thing, then hold the bright screen in front of my face to unlock it. There's a Facebook message from my first girlfriend. The girl I got kicked out of eighth grade for—the girl I wrote my first story for.

The little preview shows the beginning: *Hey Drew, sorry to reach out like this, I just wanted to let you know…*

I glance toward my sleeping wife and roll away, use my back to hide the glow. Our two-year-old wriggles, creaking the small mattress in his crib.

Hey Drew, sorry to reach out like this, I just wanted to let you know. Sam's gone. Ali wanted me to tell you. She said you guys had been talking again recently. Will send more info when I have it.

Above it are the last messages we sent each other more than a decade ago—an attempt to reconnect that went nowhere. She met her now-husband not long after. They have three children. He's a youth pastor.

I close her message and go to my last conversation with Sam, reread through it all for something I can't name.

He asked me about the air-fried salmon I posted to my story, asked if I would write the narrative for a project he was working on, would I be interested in a Friendsgiving. I was busy with kids, busy with work, busy with not being ready.

There's a patience and an earnestness to the messages I didn't see before. It could be the knowledge that he's dead, but the words are soft and kind, almost divine—a small wave from a distance, a gentle raising of the hand with a smile.

My last message to him was: *Ok.* Even still, he'd hearted it. It's like he was trying to tell me he loved me every chance he could. I tap out *I'm so sorry* and send it, a prayer into the unread ether.

I text Loam—my best friend, my son's godfather. He's already on a bus back from Hidalgo. I tell him I'll pick him up for the funeral.

I think about the number of lives we live in a decade, a year, a moment.

After we fought, harder than brothers, I hated Sam for so long it became part of me, a freckle on my shoulder that just is. The beds we lie in are filled with our former selves, the dead skin we shed each night. I'm not even the same group of cells anymore.

I tell my wife in the morning light.

"Remember my friend Sam?"

"The one who broke your teeth?"

"Yeah."

A few days later, on the way to pick up Loam, I pass by the New Orleans Center for the Creative Arts, the high school we went to together. Sam started first, then Ali, and then Loam, who went by a different name then—another life.

Sam was the one who told me to apply for the creative writing program. He'd liked the story I'd written about a lighting technician for the Nutcracker who falls in love with the lead. My first girlfriend played Clara. It's as bad as you think, but I got in.

We were the Katrina kids, parking next to piles of debris, busted for smoking weed by military police. The buildings around us spray-painted with an X to mark that they'd been searched—numbered quadrants for who searched it, when, and what they found.

The bottom of the X was for the number of bodies inside.

They're all painted over now, layered by other lives.

Loam is quiet when he gets in the car, handing me a long, orange-yellow candle. It snapped in half in his bag on the bus from Mexico. Later, I'll keep it on my mantle like an urn.

Loam tells me what he knows. Sam was killed by an eighteen-wheeler. Having stopped taking medication and relying solely on prayer, he did that thing he'd sometimes do where he disappeared, eyes wide and unblinking.

He stole his grandfather's truck in the middle of the night, drove it from Florida until it ran out of gas in Tennessee, then got out and started walking.

At some point, he crossed or ran or leapt in front of the truck and was reduced to a headline: *Florida Man Killed After Running On I-40 In Putnam County. Florida Man.* God, he would have hated that, but laughed about it.

There wasn't enough of Sam to bring home, so they're not calling it a funeral, they're calling it a celebration.

Sam's celebration is in a church that was once a youth center called One-Eighty, where, on middle-school Wednesday nights, we'd play Tekken and eat microwaved ham and cheese Hot Pockets in exchange for standing during praise and worship and sitting quietly during the sermon. A pretty solid trade.

Even then, it was Sam and Ali. Ali with her Chinese takeout box as a purse that was filled with makeup, Wrigley's spearmint gum, and Taco Bell sauce packets. She put the sauce on honeybuns, saying she wished she could bottle the smell of a Taco Bell and wear it like a perfume.

It's funny the things you remember about a person. I shared a story I wrote in my creative writing class about being molested by a neighbor, and she said I'd held her hand in third grade after the same thing had happened to her. I don't remember this at all. It's painted over.

I sit next to Loam in the back of the chapel and peel away layers of years in my mind, match faces to shapes I remember.

There's new paint and rows of royal blue fabric chairs filled with the butts of old pastors, principals, teachers, parents who didn't allow me to come to birthday parties because my parents left the church. Through them, I see the phantoms of what was once there: controllers with wobbly joysticks, a basketball cage, worn bean bag chairs with duct tape patches.

Sam's art lines the stage. Sketches, acrylic, woodwork, sculpture, portraits, landscapes, some of them incomplete, but each of them magnificent, like everything he did. His music plays softly in the background over a slideshow of photos: the wedding I wasn't invited to, friends he made after me, family, the other lives he lived.

The music stops and Ali gets up and walks to the podium.

She stops halfway through the eulogy, leaves the stage like one of his unfinished paintings. I find her in the hallway. She hugs me. Her grief is heavy hanging from my neck.

I don't remember what I tell her. Something about wishing we didn't wait until someone died to see each other. Something about how long it's been. Something everyone says.

I know what I don't tell her.

I don't tell her that the night Sam broke my teeth, our bellies full of stolen Southern Comfort, I'd told him he wasn't good enough for her.

I don't tell her that, years later, he told me I was right.

I don't tell her that he told me he was sorry, that he wanted to be better.

I don't tell her that I believed him, that I told him I loved him.

I don't tell her that I was sorry. Sorry for the decades, the years, months, weeks, moments. Sorry for everything.

A few weeks later, I meet Loam and Ali at our old high school for another celebration of life. A few people say a few words about Sam.

A stillness fills the room when they're done, and Loam gets up to speak, pulling a note out of his pocket that he'd written on the bus ride from Hidalgo. He starts to talk about how he blames the people who chose prayer over the medicine Sam so badly needed. He falters.

I stand up and put my hand on his shoulder and talk about how Sam shaped me like the clay in the sculpture room—made me who I am. How I regret holding onto a hate so fragile. How the moment I got the message that he was gone I became a different person.

The school's president talks about Sam being his first problem student.

He had challenged Sam to paint a self-portrait, which Sam did in one night, in defiance, delivering it the next day. He'd kept it in his office ever since—Sam looking down on him, forever reminding, reshaping.

He pulls down a sheet to reveal the portrait. An incredible thing. All red and black.

After the storm, the bodies at the bottom of the X were often found bloated and unrecognizable. Sometimes, they were forgotten. Sam stands with his hands in his pockets, pants splattered with paint, head slightly cocked, face serious.

Loam, Ali, and I take a picture next to it, Sam in the center and slightly above. All of us here, now, together.

July 2024

Dead Dad Joke

Chance Dibben

I can't wait for the zombie apocalypse to happen. Cause then I'll finally be able to meet my dad. (Pause for laughter).

My father's absence and the manner of his death have become mythic to me; a joke. A joke I've told many times, on stage, to strangers. Big uncomfortable laughs. Many of us comics, performing across small Midwestern stages and bars, have a dead dad joke. Nobody has one like mine.

As I level my crossbow into his eyesocket, I'll know there is a nerve, and within this nerve, a whole universe, filled with dreams and regrets. Experiences we never had. Baseball games. Shaving. Dance recitals. So many dance recitals.

The audience usually bubbles over at "dance recitals," because tension has escalated and I act out the dancing with an unexpected competency. There's a euphony in the rule of three construction here, the repetition of the long A, which I modulate through a defeated breath suggesting hidden pain. One pinch false, one pinch true.

The "experiences we never had" feel specific but aren't. My father is a void. The reality is I don't know what I missed by not having him in my life. I was not inclined toward sports or dancing growing up, though the question is if my father was around, would I have been? How different of a person would I be now? And the qualities of myself I do like, would they still be there?

It's okay. I never knew my dad. He died in a very weird way. He was an industrial baker and had to take a VAT OF DOUGH to a THING and push it up to another THING. (Linger to let audience sense what happens).

I do know he skipped town before I was born, generated another family and then abandoned them too. His relatives, cousins and the like, have connected with me online over the years, saying I look exactly like my father. They try to engage with me like the person they knew from their youth.

When my mother discovered I wrote as a child, she stopped in her tracks. "Your dad wrote songs and stories and poetry." She was worried that I was like my father. And now, I am the same age he was when he died.

"Weird way" is a weird way to describe death, and it primes the audience to anticipate the surprise. They perhaps expect an extension of the beginning, something so absurd it can't possibly be true.

The dough got STUCK so he climbed in to make it work. (Let the crowd gasp, string it out slow). Then he fucking Modern Times, Charlie Chaplin-ed that shit.

The audience is never sure what parts of the joke are true and what parts aren't, which is why I love telling the joke so much.

So now whenever I go to church and they say take this bread, my son... (linger) *for it is the body of Christ...* (linger) *I tear up a little bit. It might be my father...* (points up, lingers) *but it also might be my father (points down).*

"Welp, that's my dead dad joke," I say after the punchline. It brings the whole bit to a deflated stop, allowing the audience to catch themselves and sit with what they just heard. Other comics will use the "welp, that's my ______ joke" structure to punctuate exaggerated bits built on false premises or standard topics. Generally, though, their bits seem less over-the-top, and realer, than mine.

I've been approached many times after a show by someone in the audience wanting to know if my father really died the way I said. When I tell them yes, some offer their sympathies ("I'm so sorry for your loss"), not recognizing what I basically said on stage was that my father's death is as meaningless to me as his life. Others, I can't tell if they believe me. The bit ends on a groaner, a long walk to a dumb pun, and begins with an aggressively distorted, dark thought, so it perhaps makes sense I'd maintain the fiction post-performance.

The stage is a negotiated space, and it can be tricky to understand why you laugh at a bit. Is it the awkward truth couched in performance and exaggeration? Is it unreality, the sense that what you are told is both simultaneously true and false?

The truth (THE TRUTH) is despite the lack of connection I have to the man who I share a face and creative impulse with, I now feel guilty telling the joke. It's hard to grieve a person you never knew, but the horrifying circumstances of his death, the people that did love him, the unheard songs he wrote, they make me realize he was a person. In the abstract, I am connected more to him than I am with the facts of our biographies. I can understand him as a person who made selfish mistakes and lived a hard life. I can understand him as a creative spirit. But I cannot understand him as my father. The truth (THE TRUTH) is I keep his ghost for revenge, and this petulance will, someday, break.

I'll think about his life, in all its minutiae, void-filled, and consider what I really was doing up there on that stage.

January 2021

Kill Floor

Stephanie Austin

I needed a tampon. My father was dead. I called my mother. She gave the phone to my sister. "Dad died," I said. I wanted my sister to accept our father not as a father but as a person. I wanted him to have been a better father to both of us. I wanted us to be a family who united in grief. I wanted coffee. "Okay," she said.

We ended the call. I put my hair up, packed a shitload of tampons and ibuprofen. My mother arrived. I broke in two. Half went to my mother: a man who ruined her life was gone. Half went to my father: a victim of his own poor choices. A smoker. Lung cancer. My mother used to smoke too. I told my husband I was ready to leave, told my mother I'd check in on my daughter later in the morning. My husband drove. I called my father's brothers and sisters, some of whom answered and who were sad with me. I needed the sadness.

The caregiver shift change at my father's house happened at 6am and 6pm He died at 5:45am, and the new caregiver arrived unaware. She'd been a regular. She knew my dad for the three weeks of his dying, when his entire personality was a raspy voice and card games to pass the time. She hugged me. I peeked around her. The hospice nurse held his wrist and took his non-pulse. My aunt walked in the door—I'd left it open. More hugs. Quiet. My father was stretched out on his hospice bed in a stained white T-shirt and underwear, one stiff knee up in the air, eyes closed, mouth half open, head cocked back, chest up as though someone had tied a string around his upper body, tried to pull but failed.

Funeral home bodies are prepared and painted to be alive but asleep. Palatable. This was real death with no cover. His skin was white as the bedsheets.

"Honey," said the hospice nurse. "Do you want a moment?"

My aunt dabbed her eyes. My husband leaned against the counter.

Do I want a moment? With my father's dead body? No, I don't want a fucking moment with my father's dead body. My cramps went to an eleven. "I'm good," I said, turning my head. "I'm good. I'm good. Good. Good." The nurse asked if I was sure. "Good," I said.

I went into the kitchen. Hospice, i.e., your project coordinator, wants a funeral home on file so they can make the call when the time comes. The funeral home staff shows up with a gurney on which you will load your dead father and take him to the crematorium. The hospice nurse let me know that the Waverly Brothers were on their way. I put my hands on the counter and squeezed my eyes shut. Cramps. *Cramps.* After my daughter was born, my period was casual, light. Friendly. After I turned forty, it got nasty and unpredictable again. Everything swelled. Cramps became a three-ibuprofen-every-four-hours event. It was a kill floor.

I stood at the kitchen counter and then I felt it. A subtle yet obvious gush. A fuck you. I crossed my legs, grabbed my bag, excused myself to the bathroom, but not the hall bathroom because my dad had collapsed there last night. Bad energy. You can't change your tampon in the bathroom where your dad fell off the toilet and into the tub because the mass in his chest probably exploded. My mouth dropped. I had bled all the way through the tampon, all the way through the pad I'd put in my underwear in case the tampon failed, all the way through my underwear into my shorts. I peeled off my underwear, shoved them in my purse pocket, and swapped out the tampon. The last time I'd bled through to my shorts was in high school when I moved into my dad's house to get away from my stepfather. High school was when my dad had thousands of beers in his fridge that he let me drink once in a while. High school was when my dad and I sort of got okay for a bit. Then I noticed the laundry basket.

My dad had lost so much weight, I'd purchased several pairs of sweatpants and shorts for him. My 6' 4" father who once topped off at 210 was now in a baggy men's medium. I picked up a pair of clean black sweatshorts with a drawstring. I keyed in on a box of disposable underwear compliments of hospice. Heavy absorbency. Running short on time, I put on the disposable underwear and my dad's shorts and went back into the living room. The Waverly's had arrived.

The Waverlys were the tallest men I've ever met. I pulled my drawstring up on the cheap pants. We chatted about how their dad was a funeral home director and now they run the funeral home. Their voices were calming, low, as if the living room, now full of bright sunlight (why, my dad often asked, would a person spend money on curtains when the natural cycle of the sun was a curtain) was theirs. All four of them—the hospice nurse, the caregiver, and the two men—lifted my dad off the hospice bed and onto the gurney.

The Waverlys asked me if I wanted to walk out with the body. They asked if they should pull the sheet back so I could see his face. Like, please everyone, stop asking me if I want to gaze upon my dead father. The sun was up now. People in my father's retirement community were out walking. Garage doors were up, golf carts packed. The Waverlys closed the van, nodded. My husband and my aunt and I, in my father's disposable hospice underwear and his black drawstring shorts, stood in the driveway watching the van go until it turned the corner. My husband gave me a funny look. "Did you change?" he asked.

"Nevermind," I said.

Back inside, I peeled the DNR off his refrigerator and opened the door like it was time for breakfast. Yesterday, less than twenty-four hours ago, I filled new droppers with morphine and Ativan. Caregivers were not allowed to set meds, just administer them, and we'd gotten a new shipment. My dad was in good spirits yesterday. We sat at the table. The hospice nurse listened to his breathing, wrinkled her nose a bit. After she checked his vitals—which other than the gurgling lungs were good and normal—he stood up, said he was tired, and laid down on his hospital bed. I asked her what she thought. She said weeks. Maybe two. But she used the word weeks, not days. Not hours. Not minutes. Weeks. Hypervigilance when one's father is dying is exhausting. Weeks. I let that roll around in my brain.

From his hospice bed, he called out. The caregiver said she'd check on him. I stood in the kitchen, filled the droppers, made notes on the med chart in case whoever showed up that night was new. My father was to receive his morphine and Ativan through his feeding tube because he was refusing to take it orally. I filled droppers with Ativan. Night reports said he wasn't sleeping so they told me I could fill the syringes to the max dosage for night. I counted the vials, double checked all the amounts were correct. When I left for the night, he was dozing in his bed, and an hour after I got home, I got the call he collapsed in the hall bathroom. Now hospice was telling me that they wouldn't take back the meds. I'd touched the meds. Handled the meds. Dosed the meds. Also, don't throw meds in the trash. Also, don't flush the meds. One trick is to use a chuck (an absorbent pad). Empty all the vials into the chuck, the hospice nurse told me with her bag over her shoulder. She wished me good luck. She told me again she was sorry.

I pulled everything out of the fridge, all the vials I'd fixed up yesterday. I put gloves on because you don't want the morphine touching your skin—God forbid you get any pain relief yourself—and started emptying all the liquid into a chuck. One after another. Open, pour. Open, pour. The caregiver left. I promised I'd make sure she got paid for the day. Open, pour. The morphine would take away my cramps. Ativan for the crushing anxiety of this entire day, week, month, life. My phone rang. I answered. He's dead, I had to tell them. His remaining friends he hadn't alienated. An old girlfriend. Dead, dead. Open, pour. Phone. Dead. The Ativan teased. Just a little, it said. Just, take the edge off. Pour, pour, pour. I poured the last one.

May 2022

After Life (And A Bit Before)

Laurie Rachkus Uttich

You arrive in silence. You look up, startled and blue, a red ring around your neck. You turn toward the sound of my cry and open your mouth to protest perhaps, but an oxygen mask smothers your sounds. Scissors snap and just like that we are two and you are in the hands of the man who pulled you from me. He passes you to a woman who waits in a long white coat. She studies you; you shut your eyes.

The room shifts quickly then. A cart is pushed aside, a tray tips over. The woman holding you hurries out the door. Your arm falls to your side. Your fingers, old-bruise blue, sway and still. Your father, sobbing and sweating, follows you down the hall.

After you leave, a crowd remains. My doctor, two nurses and three others—I don't care who they are—all in surgical masks and green smocks, peer inside me. The room becomes cold, and I shake. The nurses rest latex fingers on my legs to still them. I ask if you will be all right.

The doctor stops, his needle suspended by blood-soaked fingers, looks up and finds my eyes, "We're doing everything we can."

It is then that I feel it, the fear, rising up, choking even the pain between my legs. It is then that I understand it, the seriousness of what is happening, the fact that you are fighting to breathe, the fact that you may be dying or already dead.

For a moment I think that I will vomit, that I will spew out all the terror that knits inside, but instead the room goes black.

*

My mother believes she died once. She slept in the hospital on tight sheets bleached too white. My father made us waffles for dinner while her body hummed, alive with worry. Her hysterectomy left a space and something protested. A vein collapsed and blood seeped, unchecked, a swollen river without a shore.

There was a chill, she says, felt only by the warmth that tiptoed behind. She rose from her bed. She looked down at her body. She realized she was prettier than she had known. And she could breathe, full deep breaths that made her buoyant.

There was a light—there always is—and she followed it. A tunnel formed, she knows it sounds trite, but she still says today, over thirty years ago, it made her float. She followed that light, in that tunnel, and stopped in a place brighter, but sweeter than the sun.

She prepared to rest, she says, to unfold like a blanket thrown over sand from the sea. She felt large and full, and there was no pain and no worry and no thought of the nutritional value of waffles at dinnertime. She started to stretch, a woman free of clothes too tight, heels too high, and then she thought, "But what about Gina and Laurie?"

A bolt, a slash of pain: she winces even now describing it to me. "And then I was just so heavy, so trapped, my pockets full of bricks." She looks at me hard, weighing my worth, considering her choice. I don't think she's ever forgiven us.

The doctors say her heartbeat stopped for four minutes. My sister, Gina, says Mom's always been a bit insane.

*

The frog is perfect. He is still and pale green, a shade two leaves from the core of a head of lettuce. He sits in the driveway by our garage.

"Ooooh, he's so cuuuute," says my second son, Zack, just three. He bends to pet it, one dirty finger reaching out to its back. It does not move, and I look closer.

"Wait, honey, don't touch it," I say.

He pulls his hand back fast. "It bite?"

I shake my head. "No, it's dead."

"Dead?" he asks, and I kneel down, too, place his hand over his heart.

"Do you feel that?" a quiet pump beneath a dinosaur T-shirt. He nods, not sure.

"It's your heart," I tell him, his breath close to mine. "And the frog had one, too, but now it doesn't work and when that happens, it means he's dead."

"Dead," he says.

"Yes."

"He jump?" he says, and I sigh just a little.

"No, the part of him that jumped and played and ate flies is gone now."

"Oh." A silence. He weighs the worth of this frog and says, "His Mommy sad?"

I do not know the heart of a frog, but I do know that the path to a frog begins with two hundred eggs, fewer tadpoles, and then, a long lonely process in a damp place. The frog, finally formed, then hops away. I doubt he remembers to call home.

"Yes," I say. "His Mommy's sad."

We both take a moment, pay our respects.

Then, "I keep him?"

I picture Zack's closet, his box with feathers, rocks, a square piece of a snake, evidence of a lawn-mower murder. It is the perfect resting space for a skeleton of a frog, but not a corpse that beckons to bugs. "No, honey, he belongs to the sun and the sky and the dirt and the wind. They're still a part of him. They'll take care of him."

Zack stands then, looks at me. "He be cold."

I stand, too, put my hand on his shoulder and feel the bones beneath his shirt. How easily he could break, almost as weak as a frog left in the Florida heat. "He can't anymore. He can't be cold or hungry or sad or have owies anymore. Nothing can hurt him now."

He nods. We watch him for a while and consider this absence of discomfort. Too much perhaps for a boy with two skinned knees, a bruise on his elbow. Then, "No sads? No more?"

I rub his hair with the palm of my hand. "No sads, no more."

He nods again, considers. "I kick him?"

I hesitate. "I guess so. But just to the grass."

*

You are four hours old and no longer blue. Hands bring you to me, place you in my arms, arrange the tube taped to your mouth. We are both awake now and we look hard at each other.

My tears fall on your face, but neither of us blinks.

I study you. I breathe you. I have never felt so much and so little like an animal.

Then, I realize it, this simple truth: we have loved each other before. I know you like I know the freckle at the base of my wrist, the attic of my childhood home, the curve of your father's chin. *I know you.* This knowing is not like the face in a crowd that you look at too long, wondering where you've met before. It is like the hidden cellar beside your Grandmother's home. You grow—your youth a memory—and return one day, a guest where everything is and is not familiar. You go to the cellar, you open the door in the ground, you step down, inside the dirt, reach out your hand into the dark and there, *there*, your fingers awake and remember: the jars of jam, the bin of potatoes, the candle on the shelf, the matches behind the stewed tomatoes... everything just the way you left it. You remember, even in the dark. You *know.*

Years will pass, and one day I will have two other sons, and they will be as loved, but you are the only one that I have known at the break of birth.

*

My Uncle Bud is dying, and he's taking a long time to do it. My mother, his sister, says he was always that way, doing things the hard way.

We are on our way to visit him at the nursing home ("No, Laurie Ann, the long-term care facility. For God's sake, don't say 'nursing home' to him"). I am driving, my license one week old. My mother makes us take the back roads, they wind and curve, and old Illinois oaks cloak every comer in surprise. But it's safer for a new driver, my mother tells me. Everyone else is on that interstate.

I drive the way Jimmy Carter says I should to save gas and lives, as slow as I can. I wish away time. I am only coming to see my Uncle Bud because my mother let me drive.

I think of the last time we saw my uncle, his eyes half closed on a bed shut still with metal bars. He struggled when he saw us, pulled himself up to a slump on straight pillows. He waved his three fingers at us—two lost in the door of a fire truck a decade or so before—and motioned me over, "Look! Pull that sheet up, kiddo. See what they did to my goddamn leg."

A blurred brown bandage was wrapped around the space where his leg once stood. His thigh, an orphan, looked too thin, underfed. I looked away, pulled the sheet back. "Ouch," I said, too soft. His face shifted then, lost and gained more years than I had been alive, and he began to cry, long wails that sounded like a joke at first.

My mother motioned me out of the room, a flick of her wrist. I backed away from the bed.

Later, I stood by the door, listened to the even tone of my mother, a mix of murmured words all in tune. Every now and then I would hear my uncle, as loud as when he was drunk, and then, "Shit, sis, I'm scared to death. All the shit I pulled, you can't know."

But my mother does know. She made tea for my aunt the first time he hit her. My mother kept his children for a summer, watched my father teach them chess. She told my aunt sometimes even Catholics have to get divorced.

My mother knows the shit he pulled—believes in the Hell he fears—but still she says, "Do you remember that time when there was no money, and Dad had to do the one thing that could make a man hate him: cross the picket line? Do you remember what Mom said when they bombed our house and all the kids were wailing, 'We're going to die'? She said we are promised eternity and we are, Bud, we are."

Today, when we will visit him, he will tell my mother that their brothers, both dead for many years, have come to see him. He will tell her, "They keep bugging me to go with them; they never let the hell up."

My mother will plead, "Why don't you go, Bud? Why not?"

He won't answer, and we won't ask him anything else, but years later when we tell family ghost stories, we will tell this one and forget to say that on the day Uncle Bud saw his brothers, he also thought my mother was his mother, that I was the nurse, that his leg was whole, his infection a sunburn after a Fourth of July picnic with his ten-year-old son who had been married and living in Chicago for fifteen years.

*

You do not die. You are not even wounded much. Your bruises soften and fade, your breath grows strong and even. Your throat heals, your mind whirls. You grow, you love, you learn, you lie and cry, you consume me, perfect a part of me. Everything that shook your birth is stilled; nothing but the loud life of you remains.

Tonight we drive away from my parents' home, along an Illinois highway where even in the black, fields lie down like pancake batter in a pan. Everyone but you sleeps while I drive. You are seven now, and you want to know how four girls can die in a fire. "But two of them ride my bus," you say, and I cry without notice or noise.

You are worried that they are in Heaven without their parents. You go through it again. "I just don't understand how it can happen. How did the mom and dad get out of the house and the kids didn't?" It makes no sense to you, a child the center of his own universe.

I try to explain the seductiveness of smoke, how it taunts and teases you, stumbles you into a stray sleep. "And then when that man drove by and saw the fire, he ran to the first room in the house, and that's where the parents were sleeping."

You sigh, annoyed. "*I know.* But I don't understand why they didn't tell him where the kids were."

"When they were outside—when the wind woke them and the smoke cleared from their brains—then they *did* tell him. They remembered, and they tried to run into the house, even though it was really burning then and the firefighters were there. It was just too late."

You are quiet, considering, and I think about the newspaper article, the mother screaming, "My babies are in there, my babies! Please, God, get my girls!"

Our lives push us past the spot where that house once stood. Publix, the pediatrician, play group, the gas station with the French Vanilla coffee... the house stands between us and them. Almost every day we drive by. We watch it in silence, study the shell and later the flattened plot, and I tell myself, "Enough, you cannot cry again. Enough."

Weeks pass, but even now the road blurs, and I blink too hard. You don't even pretend not to notice, but still I lie to myself and say all my tears are for the girls mugged of life and for the mother who stumbles into that dark space—the death of her children—and crawls out with only the curse of her own life. I tell myself that not one of these tears is for me, for the fear that grows beside you, the fear that you or one of your brothers will be lost, hurt, altered, stolen, amputated from me.

The fear that I will live and one of you will die.

Tonight, you are not satisfied. "*You* would come get me," you say, seven-year-old sure. "Dad would, too."

I want to say, "Yes, of course, we would, how could we not?" but I cannot do that to the mother who lives. "Oh, honey. You can't know how much they wished they could have."

You think a minute, look out the window, weigh your words under the cover of the night. You are about to say something awful and maybe true, and you know it. "I think they just didn't want to be dead, too."

"Oh, baby," I say, and I do not sigh, not even a little. "No, I don't think so. I think they would rather be dead than have to live without their children."

But you have said the awful words, and now the gate is open. "No, they wouldn't," you tell the window. "And now their kids are in Heaven by themselves."

I want to tell you my truth that Heaven is wherever there is love, but you are in your own space now, that place where you have decided what is and what is not. "Grandma says that God called them home, that He was lonely for them, for more little angels."

I do not turn around or glance into my mirror. I look ahead into the dark and think about my God. She is bigger, but perhaps less powerful than my mother's God. Her God is a noun; mine a heartbeat of a verb. My God wept when the air conditioner cord separated, spit and sparked. Her God could have stopped it.

I no longer pretend not to cry. "I don't know, honey." I do not know about lonely angels, Uncle Ghosts, the separation of saints and sinners, but I do believe those girls followed my mother's light, their souls stepping over the boundaries of their bodies. I believe this—tonight I do—and still I think that I would trade my life for theirs, easy math, one woman not-quite young for four lives not-quite lived. And perhaps I would shrink, the gun cold in my mouth, the flames at my feet, even the loss of light in your motherless eyes, but tonight it seems simple. I have sighed with a coral reef at the bottom of the sea, peered over the tips of two skis at the top of a mountain, inhaled five hundred years of hushed holiness in the stone walls of a church. I have awakened, full and warm, to find a man I love has watched me sleep. I have matched words the way I wanted to; formed webs of friendship that weave around the corners of my life, connecting me whole; and felt joy, sticky and syrup sweet, fill three boys who jump and sing when I walk in the room. It is not enough—not nearly yet—but my scale dips full next to four girls, the oldest just nine. How could I tell this to you? How do you turn and nod at death and still lock hands with life? How do I explain—or excuse—a belief with no real basis or proof? How do I describe a homing device that may just be a masquerade for hope?

"I don't want to be in Heaven without you," you say, and I can hear the tears in your own voice. "I don't want to go by myself. You'll go with me, right? You will. Right?"

Beside you two babies sleep. My life is not my own to lose. And even if it was, could I do that to my spirit? Even if the loss of you left me not half whole, would I? Or would I wait, let the world spin and end, half-sure that I would meet you yet again?

You ask me to pinky swear, the most solemn of seven-year-old oaths.

I pull over and turn in my seat. I look you right in the eyes. "Yes," I tell you. "I will die of a broken heart and go with you." It is our first big lie. You hold out your littlest finger. I clasp it with my own. We form a sacred circle, knuckles and nails. You nod, satisfied, and I pull back onto the road and drive into the darkness.

December 2020

LIFE

Say You're Pregnant

Holly Pelesky

Say you just found out you're pregnant, after your second time having sex.

You were raised to be a virgin until marriage, then a wife, then a mother.

When you hear the voicemail from your brother saying, "Mom and dad know," you climb into your car and decide you will drive far away, change your name maybe, work in a filling station in Wyoming or Montana or South Dakota. But the January mountains stop you. You turn the car around.

You sit on the couch and cry when your mom asks how this happened. You explain what you've been up to at college: not Bible studies and church services but drinking your nights away after working doubles at the restaurant.

She asks you what it's like to be drunk. She's never had even a sip of alcohol. Tell her it's like being someone else. But don't tell her that it's like being someone closer to yourself, someone you weren't raised to be.

She says you're moving back in with her for the duration of your pregnancy. And since you will be living at her house again, you will be going to church each week. You don't resist, even though you want to. You've disobeyed enough already.

You post your apartment on Craigslist, quit your job, fax your résumé to a restaurant close to your parents' house. It doesn't take long until you run out of money. You get a job at a café that serves quiche and sandwiches and mochas. You work weekend mornings, so you no longer have to bother with church. Mostly, the clientele are people visiting dying loved ones in hospice next door.

Your mother expects you to keep the baby, to stay living at home, to raise it with her help. The adoption agency gives you a second batch of profiles, and there is a couple you know immediately is the right one.

You keep working at the café, your belly growing and growing, your belt dropping lower and lower beneath it. This small thing of making lattes and slicing cakes and delivering quiche to tables of grieving people makes you feel useful.

You find out your baby is a girl. Tears slip from your cheeks on the examination table while the ultrasound technician talks excitedly about your baby as if you'll keep her.

The adoption agency throws you a shower. Your college roommate, writing professor, a waitress you work with, and your daughter's mother show up and give you gifts.

It's getting hot; it's summer, and you're huge with child and bloat.

You show up to the hospital on time. After a workday of labor, she is born. A nurse brings her to you, swaddled, only her face peeking out. Her red blotchy cheeks look like yours.

You try not to cry.

You cry, even though you tried so hard not to.

When you watch your daughter's mother hold her, you look away.

You count down the hours, no the minutes, until it's over: the torturous forty-eight hours you have to change your mind and keep the baby.

You tell your daughter's parents they can name her.

They pick *Grace.*

You call her Gracie instead. Like she's yours. Like you have any say in who she becomes.

Ten days after she is born, you move away. On your way out of the state, you stop at her house over the Cascade Mountains. She's so much bigger already, her cheeks are full. She has reddish skin and blond hair and blue eyes, just like you. And you love her.

Say you will live without each other.

Say you climb into your Saturn loaded down with your belongings and back down the drive.

Say you wave.

Say you leave.
Say you leave.
Say you leave.
Say you've left your daughter.
Clutching the wheel, you convince yourself you'll try to go on.
You don't know what the hell that means.
But say you try.

March 2021

Reprise

Claire Hopple

Let's be clear: I don't know anything about music. And I don't want to come off as dramatic, but a local DJ changed my life. By that I mean I'd been floundering. Getting ready in the morning is rough enough as it is, and when you want to play a little something to make the experience a tad more bearable, you need to depend on a trove of songs that will get you there. But I didn't have that.

The DJ played a few tracks from Little Richard's *Southern Child.*

This album was scheduled to release in 1972, the same year it was recorded, but Reprise Records shelved it.

Once he passed away, amid the height of the pandemic, somebody decided to finally let it come up for air. Yes, Little Richard made a country western album.

If I had to guess I'd say the label was embarrassed by it. I smirked when the DJ introduced it. Then I listened to it. Now I can't stop playing it.

Why shouldn't Little Richard have a country western album? Why was that amusing to me? Why didn't I take it seriously? Why didn't the label even take it seriously?

Granted, there are songs that don't age well. Like when he compares his old girlfriend to a racehorse or explains how dogs bark across the globe through ethnocentrically cringy descriptions. However, the guy really can do it all, and now I'm fully embracing his range.

Back in eighth grade, a classmate of mine committed suicide. I never knew him. His face didn't even look familiar. That might have been part of the problem. Apparently he was bullied. I'm sure there's a lot more to the story.

That year was the apex of physical awkwardness for me. I was caught up in the same things every pubescent peer was caught up in. I had friends and crushes and after-school activities that sort of took over, and it was overwhelming and terrible and downright fantastic.

Our middle school Chorus teacher was somehow asked if she could pull a performance together for this boy's funeral.

The only thing we had practiced was "When You Believe" from *Prince of Egypt,* an animated movie about the biblical Exodus. Mariah Carey and Whitney Houston popularized it.

Anyway, that's what we had to go with. And we did. We sang about miracles while a boy's family stared blankly ahead and a Catholic priest prepared to speak about a child who ended his own life. (As a Presbyterian, I knew enough to know that most Catholics think suicide automatically translates to Hell. Us Protestants didn't make such declarations.)

I saw Little Richard once, about five years ago, in Nashville's Hillsboro Village. He was hanging out the back of an Escalade, greeting bystanders, tooling down the road. Maybe he was preemptively saying goodbye, the cancer chewing up his bones.

Regardless, Little Richard was waving to his subjects. He was gracing us all with his royal—and originally rural—presence.

September 2022

Five Years Before the First Lady Launched Her Be Best Campaign

Teresa Carmody

I moved to Colorado and began living like the graduate students I'd long envied. I bought a table and bookshelf at Ikea, then hung a crystal in my window, so every morning, rainbow spots danced across the plain walls of the studio apartment I'd rented in what some called the popular neighborhood. The university was near the mountains, in a city that boasted of its altitude. Everyone there liked to drink, and the lack of oxygen increased the alcohol's impact on the body, so one drink felt like two, and two effected four. In this way, it was easy to become quite drunk.

I had just turned thirty-seven years old, the first irregular prime, but during that first year in Colorado, I frequently had hangovers like I did when I was fifteen in Western Michigan and would binge drink Bacardi 151 in a light blue Volkswagen rabbit with three other girls, one of whom was usually my friend. We drank in the parking lot of an all-ages dance club, Top of the Rock, always on Thursdays, alternative night, where we could meet other punks, skaters, and still-closeted teen queers, our bodies thrumming with everything we could not say or see for fear of eternal damnation and abandonment. In high school, the hangovers began the next day at school, a headache settling in during third or fourth period, which meant only a few hours of misery before I could nap at home, pleased that I had not been caught by my religious mother. In Colorado, the hangovers sometimes stretched into early evening when I would finally and gingerly take the dogs for a walk at the nearby park, worrying, as I often did, that I had wasted my day sleeping and aching instead of reading and writing. I would sigh, then, about my lack of friends and invitations, my headache wrapped in a familiar accusation of being not enough. Except for when I was too much: too tense, too critical, too desirous. And then I was feeling sorry for myself, another no-no as no one, not even a mother, likes a whiner.

I remember mine standing before the make-up mirror she kept on the tall bedroom dresser, her pale face glowing from the pink filtered lights set into the mirror's sides. She was applying eye shadow and blush for a rare evening out; maybe she was going with my father to a Buick Club meeting at the pancake restaurant, while I was trying to tell her of my loneliness. I was six or seven years old, and my older siblings, all four of them, did not like me. They called me annoying, selfish, gullible, weird. They would not let me join their board games or sit under the blanket with them as they whispered scary stories in the dark. *You're too sensitive,* they said. No one likes me, I confided to my mother, who paused, leaned over, her bright eyes even brighter. *Self-pity,* she whispered, *is a sin.*

I did not want to be a sinner.

Later, when I wrote a story about that memory, I let the mother invite her daughter to the Buick Club meeting where the mother hated herself while making small talk with the other women while the men drank and spoke cars and the daughter, the only child present, ordered blueberry pancakes with whipped cream and became, by herself, a giant-mouthed God, punishing each berry for its blueness.

*

In Colorado, I began eating like the locals. I bought dried foods from bulk bins at the natural grocery store, filled cloudy plastic bags with trail mix, granola, wasabi peas, and organic popcorn. The graduate program was in writing and literature, and knowing my own proclivity for pettiness, I tacked a note on the inside of my apartment door, which I sometimes read before leaving, though not when I was hungover and taking out the trash or checking the laundry in the basement. Those times I barely remembered my keys and quarters, much less to pause before the 3x5 notecard where I'd written, in black sharpie: *Remember the best parts.*

Because my tendency, I knew, was to fixate on the problems. Like one of my classmates, a young white man nearly two decades my junior who declared Pope Paul John II his intellectual hero and whose research focused on Flannery O'Connor, as she was Southern and Catholic. Like him. We were in the same entering cohort and had at least one literature course together every semester, where he argued with everything we read, not to better understand what the writer meant, but to measure his interpretation of the text against his idea of moral righteousness and capital-T truth. I recognized a younger version of myself in this behavior, for I, too, had worried about moral pollution and how environments seep into you, so that even as I was inexplicably drawn to lesbians, non-binary feminists, and artsy queers, I had for years attributed my own gay arousals to influence rather than an intuitive self-knowing. Sadly, my classmate was not gay, which may help to explain why he found the church a more comfortable fit. He was also fond of St. Augustine, quoting this man with great regularity, and while I never asked my classmate directly, I suspect he embraced Augustine's idea of original sin as embodied fact rather than a fiction imagined during a time when the Catholic church was solidifying its empire and needed methods of subjugation. If they get inside your head, they can rule you from the inside out; make people believe they are worthless, and they will attach themselves to the person or institution declared the best-and-only-worthy, thus offering their energetic life force, freely it seems, toward this best-and-only-worthy's increased power and gain. In the classroom, this young man always had a question or comment, and when he spoke, the other students shifted in their seats as a dispersed and unfocused atmosphere filled the room. Sometimes, I argued with the young man. One time, I told him to stop talking. But usually, like the other students, I disengaged.

Later, I wondered if he played this role for us, became a primary distraction and excuse for ceding the learning space and thus avoiding more vulnerable or difficult questions, ones we could not answer or maybe even articulate. Am I lovable? From whence comes my real authority? What is true but not mutually exclusive? The young Catholic gave us someone to hate, or more accurately, he gave me someone to hide behind and gossip about as I rolled my eyes at his narrow views and exuded sense of white "innocence." He appeared so out of step with the times that he became, in some ways, like the buffoonish celebrity running for president—another person I did not take seriously, for surely that would not be our future. Such blatant racism and sexism were too frowned upon, I erroneously thought, and how could an entertainer with no government experience win the highest political office in the land. So as my young, conservative classmate compared and contrasted his own theological notions against the writings of Maurice Blanchot or Herman Melville, the rest of us doodled, checked our email, fantasized about a large raven pecking his head. And all too often, the classroom conversation became a back and forth between this young man and—given the faculty demographics of this and many English departments—a white male professor, possibly well-intentioned, often middle-aged. A professor who might have known something was off, but not how to fix it. A teaching professor who became grateful, even, for this one student he could count on for in-class discussions. The young man who always had something to say.

June 2022

Five Weddings

Kevin Maloney

The first time my wife and I got married, a global pandemic spread across the earth, shutting down civilization. With nothing to do but rub our avocados with Clorox wipes, we started bickering about things like—is it safe to eat avocados rubbed with Clorox wipes? In a moment of whimsy, we drove to the desert and stood in the sun with our four best friends and got married on the dry spiderwebbed mud. My wife's dress was see-through. The photographer said, "I feel like a pornographer." I said, "I hope you got the money shot." Afterwards, all the guests soaked in geothermal hot springs, and the traumatized photographer went home. Eventually, my wife and I snuck off and consummated our marriage in a metal trailer without air conditioning, pausing occasionally to make sure neither of us had heat stroke.

Our second wedding was a year later. Our friends and family drove across America to be there. Nobody cared about the pandemic anymore. We said our vows, and everybody clapped, and then we slow danced to a Townes Van Zandt song. At one point, my wife whispered, "I feel like all of this has happened before." I said, "What are you doing next Tuesday?"

Our third wedding was the following Tuesday. We'd spent two years planning and having weddings and didn't know how to do anything else. We drove to the courthouse. The clerk said, "According to our files, you're already married."

We said, "Yeah, we know."

The clerk said, "You need to get divorced if you want to get married again."

We said, "That is literally the opposite of our vows."

We got mad and went outside. There was a protest. We joined in and waved our fists, demanding justice for all the suffering people of the world.

At one point, a police officer arrested us. We said, "Wait, will you marry us first?"

He said, "I'm not a priest."

We said, "Close enough."

He said, "By the power invested in me..." as he handcuffed us with zip ties.

Our fourth wedding was the following winter. The pandemic was back. They let us out of jail. We were free people who couldn't go anywhere because all the businesses were closed again. It rained every day. Our street flooded, and we watched salmon migrate and spawn from our living room window.

My wife said, "I'm bored. We should get married."

I said, "Our friends must be getting sick of all these weddings."

She said, "Our weddings are literally the only thing happening right now."

We fashioned a boat from the discarded arbor we built for Wedding #2 and floated around the city, visiting friends.

They said, "Cool boat. You aren't getting married again, are you?"

We said, "We're still in love. We can't help it."

They got dressed up and followed us in inner tubes that we towed behind us using an intricate system of ropes and zip ties that the police used to handcuff us in Wedding #3. We floated out to sea, where we were married in international waters by a foul-mouthed ship captain who asked us, "Do ye salty lovebirds swear to adore each other in stormy waters and in fair? In mutiny and in bounty?" We said, "Aye aye."

Our fifth wedding was last week. We were lying in bed watching *The Bachelorette.* It was hometowns. One of the contestants, Bryan, took the bachelorette on a merry-go-round, then introduced her to his cranky uncle Henry. Later, Bryan said, "I'm not just *falling* in love with you. I'm *in love* with you."

My wife said, “This show’s stupid.”

I said, “It’s the best.”

She said, “Did we sound like that when we were falling in love?”

I said, “No, we were cool.”

There was a commercial, so we decided to get married. Our cat officiated. We put a copy of the *Tao Te Ching* in front of him. We consummated the marriage before the show came back on. Afterwards, we started planning our next wedding.

My wife said, “We gotta up the ante. Hear me out. Space?”

I said, “I’m thinking the opposite. A wedding so tiny that nobody realizes it’s happening. Not even us.”

My wife just looked at me. Eventually, she said, “Isn’t that just… being married?”

I said, “I guess so.”

That’s when it occurred to us. It was time to do something else. We held each other as the weight of our non-wedding lives crashed down on us, trying to pull us apart.

November 2022

Unfinished

Abigail Oswald

After Angela Carter died at fifty-one, her executor discovered the synopsis for a *Jane Eyre* sequel folded away in a drawer. I have remained fascinated with this unwritten book since I first heard of it, owing to a longstanding personal obsession with unfinished projects: sprawling works that exist only in fragment, as typed notes or handwritten pages, or an idea tucked into a corner of someone's mind. For some time now, I have wanted to write about the book that Carter never had the chance to begin.

I've written this essay over and over. The previous paragraph carries through each draft, introducing you to my obsession, providing context—and from there it inevitably devolves.

*

Instead of writing, I look out the window. Each sentence takes minutes. I write a word and then stare off into space. Another word, another minute.

A hardcover copy of Carter's biography sits on my desk, guilting me. She looms on the cover, reproduced beautifully in black and white; she watches me write and send emails and work on everything but this essay with her two unblinking eyes.

I'd meant to read *The Invention of Angela Carter* from start to finish, as biographer Edmund Gordon likely intended. Instead, I dip in and out, consuming random sections of her life before putting the book back down again. I don't want to read about her lung cancer or her death. Biographies of the dead always fill me with a sense of foreboding, as I am unable to shake the gloom of what I am reading toward. My achronological reading habit acts as a kind of protection, allowing me to read in a state where Carter is perpetually alive—sometimes younger, sometimes older, but never gone.

Of the sequel, Gordon writes that Carter was "planning to recover" after finishing a course of radiotherapy; it was during this time that the novel was pitched. We are given the bare bones of a story that Carter imagined would run 50,000 words. The novel would have followed Rochester's ward, Adela, on a dark and twisted path of romance that smacks of the Electra complex.

It strikes me, returning again to the index, that the full discussion of this unwritten novel is located on page 404 in the hardcover: classic internet shorthand for "Page Not Found."

*

I reread Carter's Wikipedia page. At the time of this writing, the entry says the following of the *Jane Eyre* sequel: *only a synopsis survives*. As if the book itself had been a living entity.

In the internet age, nothing is more discouraging than the realization that you have found every piece of information that exists about something online. I'm no stranger to this problem; I have scraped the final pages of many a Google search, been failed by the Wayback Machine time and again. I have read the executor's *Guardian* article, the biographer's commentary, every one-line synopsis and speculative blog post.

The book itself does not exist. I allowed myself to prolong this realization for some time, living in a kind of alternate universe where the book simply had yet to be found, existing as a handwritten manuscript in a forgotten dusty box in someone's attic. That would make for a better story, wouldn't it?

*

I google images of Carter, scrolling the consequent gallery. I have long since memorized her particular smile, the black-and-white lines of her cheekbones, the variant pairs of oversized glasses. I feel as if I could draw her from memory.

Did she identify more with Jane or with Bertha, I wonder? *Jane Eyre* is a book that people often develop deep, personal attachments to. It feels like a personality quiz just waiting for you to begin: Are you Jane? Or are you the madwoman in the attic?

I studied *Jane Eyre* during my undergraduate degree. I spent hours driving between cities back then; the people I loved were spreading themselves further apart from each other, and I accumulated countless hours in transit before my graduation. I listened to a *Jane Eyre* audiobook on one of these trips; the resulting experience would print itself indelibly within my mind as one of motion.

*

Instead of writing this essay, I make a list of reasons why I shouldn't.

I haven't finished the biography. I should reread *Jane Eyre* first. I don't know everything there is to know about Angela Carter. I have not personally seen the proposal for the unwritten *Jane Eyre* sequel. And I am not a nonfiction writer!

I say this last one adamantly to myself, attaching an exclamation point. Upon initially writing this, I am apparently very sure of it. Upon returning to it, I question the exclamation point and the confidence it implies.

As if the nonfiction narrative is not just another way of telling a story. As if we do not all, every day, share the narratives of our lives with each other. Perhaps the mere act of transcribing an obsession is a kind of nonfiction. Maybe what I have to do to finish the essay is make you understand why I am obsessed with this book that was never written. But I am still not entirely sure of the answer myself.

Can you finish a project without yet knowing what it is about? Or is it the act of completion that finally communicates this to the writer? Does the understanding in some cases come after the completion, even the publication?

Am I writing this for you, or for myself?

*

There is a story I have been working on since grad school. I add whole sections. I take them out. I write elaborate backstories that are never included in any form. Whole scenes that no one else will ever read. I submit the story in different forms and it receives varying degrees of rejection.

It's finished! I have thought at least a hundred times. The exclamation point again. And then I open the document once more: an hour later, a week later. Months. But I always return.

Maybe we can think of unwritten stories not as incomplete works, but their own kind of form, of genre. Narratives that have yet to be transcribed. The *yet* feeling more hopeful than *never*. The idea that Carter's story still exists somewhere out in the ether, merely waiting to be written down.

Or maybe when we are obsessed with something, the project can never be finished. A publication only ever a stop along the way rather than an endpoint. A writer once told me at a reading that she wanted to take her book off the shelf and keep going, keep adding, keep making changes. There was still so much she had to say.

I myself have difficulty looking back at my earlier published work, returning to the old obsessions with new eyes. Perhaps we are all leaving a trail of ourselves, our evolutions not just as writers but as people, and this is part of the point—not saying what we want to say with perfect clarity, but depicting a process of creative evolution. Like shedding husks digitally, a trail across the internet marking iterations of our earlier selves.

*

In a perfect world, I could end this essay with the discovery of a completed manuscript, a sheaf of pages in the attic. But many artists die before their time. Many projects are never finished. We mourn not just this one unwritten book, but the ideas that Carter could have had over the next fifty years if she had lived—the things she hadn't even begun to think of yet.

I went through a phase where I was adamant about the existence of the multiverse. I still like to think that somewhere out there exists a universe where Carter is still alive. Where she finished her sequel to *Jane Eyre.* Where Charlotte Brontë herself didn't die at thirty-eight. Where I wrote the version of this essay I envisioned when I put pen to paper for the first time, the idea the newest and freshest that it would ever be. A universe where no one dies until they have said every last thing they want to say.

February 2022

UNVANISHING

Beth Kephart

Watching the birds through the bedroom windows. The zip-velocity of their flight into the berry tree on the eastern edge of the lawn. The eclipsing of their feathers inside the skim of green.

The sun is fur behind fog.

The near air is steam.

*

After my father died and stories left me, I wanted paper, color, thread, ephemera. I don't mean to poeticize my sudden vacancy. I want only to say that I grew to need the weight of the brayer, the blade, the awl in my hands, the bone folder and the needle. That I would wake early and climb out of bed and descend into the kitchen where, on a portable island beneath a warming bulb, I'd squeeze color from tubes onto a crusty gelli plate and fit what I made into the frame of our one table. I would fold, sew, Washi tape. I would slice squares into triangles and edge triangles into squares. Purple sticks of glue. Sticky fingers.

After, I would drink my ginger tea while my husband drank espresso.

*

The birds vanish. They unvanish. The heat is white, and rinsing.

*

I bought Stonehenge paper, Arches paper, bright sulfite, facile newsprint. I bought multiples of the same waxed linen thread because I liked the way hope beat in me when new spools arrived in cellophane. I painted cards. I chain-stitched journals. I sent what I made to my father's friends, and then to friends who had known my father, and then to friends who had not known my father, and then to strangers who did not know me; that is: I filled the mailboxes of neighbors.

It went on like this. Fall, then winter.

*

I wonder if birds always know what they want. If they know what knowing is.

*

Alyson answered the lonesomeness I had not known to name. I am not good at gifts, is what she claimed, but her gift—Bhutan Edgeworthia paper of magnificent density—straight broke me. Yellow Tsharsho. Bleached White Tsharsho. Khenpa Tsharsho. Indigo Tsharsho. Tong Fu Tsharsho. Chu Tsharsho. An incomparable luxury.

I designed new shapes of books to honor the gift I had received. New stitchings. I ordered paper made from the Huun tree. Fuschia. Navy. Deep green. On the day the box was due to come I waited at the door, impatiently.

*

Ruta asked me to explain. I fumbled the vocabulary.

*

In time, we rearranged the house so that I'd have room to work. Given more space, there was more need. Sharper blades and whole families of awls and stitches growing in complexity. How many scissors do you need? How many rulers? How much paper? How much greed to make the thin, blank things?

*

The birds plucking their berries from their tree.

*

In an old barn shelved with split peach crates, I found a book of Russian phrases, and a dictionary of foreign terms, and *Assembly Songs for School and College*. I bought these for my decoratives. At a flea market on a bitter day, I bought Grimm tales illustrated by Maurice Sendak and the Maxfield Parrish iteration of *Arabian Nights*. I turned my duplicate of Virginia Woolf's *Diary Volume One* into material. My auxiliary copies of *Mrs. Jack* and *A Certain Climate*. I bought but could not slice into use the air-mail letters of last-century war widows.

*

I collected the leaves of gingko trees, tulip trees, toxic nandina. The cold leather of rhododendron leaves. The soft brush of winterized grasses. I pressed what I'd gathered onto gelli-plated color, lay down a sheet of Arches, and used my fist. Stopped fisting. Peeled.

That was my negative.

I removed the leaves, returned the paper. Fisted harder.

That was my positive.

I never got what I expected.

*

I wonder if the berries on the backyard tree would be classified, in the pharmacy of birds, as hallucinogens. I wonder because lately the birds in the rinsing heat have grown excessive in their frantic. They vanish and unvanish with flustering speed. Sometimes, flustering back out into the world, they strike my windowpanes. I rush from the bed to the window and look down, to the ground, to see if they've survived. They survive, shaking the bruise out of their feathers.

*

I bought khadi paper, bark paper, embossed ficus leaves. Kozo paper, bodhi leaf paper, chongco flower paper. More waxed linen. More needles—longer, thinner, sensually curved—until Katrina, working by the light of her blue and golden mountain, took fabric culled from distant lives to make me a pincushion. Unheralded, her box arrived. I opened it, astounded.

*

Bill shaped and baked clay beads, sizing the holes so they would accommodate my needles. He ordered me miniature brass keys and 1928 pharmacy scripts from the Peoples Drug Store in Abingdon, Virginia. He said maybe I could use these things in the blank books I was making, then he left me precisely where I had been standing, maundering adjectives.

*

Then Carolyn sent a box of bookbinding clamps, and a story. After that, she sent a papermaker's frames and screens, tufts of old paper still wedged between them. She sent a bag of crisp dried flowers and instructions on color fasting.

Then Ruta remembered a time when she and her brother and sister all lived in LA and traveled, on Sunday mornings, to the Rose Bowl flea market. She'd been searching for books, she said, and found buttons instead, hundreds of them snug in an oblong, nine-inch heavy cardboard Hershey Kisses Chocolate container. A rare delicacy of a box in hues of pink-silver and old-denim blue containing thousands, maybe ten thousand, maybe ten million buttons. Which she sent to me in a box that smelled of smoke, along with two Nancy Drew books, published 1949 and 1959, and the brown stuff of old tapped-out Western Union paper: *Leaving seven fifty tonight arrive Chicago seven forty five tomorrow night via Northwestern.*

Then Claire said, I will show you zinnias.

Then Mark said, Come to my garden. Steal my flowers.

*

It's been nearly a year since my father died. The birds vanish, they unvanish, I am watching. They take what they need. They return when they can. The sun leaves the fog. The near steam rises.

February 2022

Five Ways of Looking at a Cockroach

Diana Ruzova

1. With disgust

One night in the shower, after a few glasses of wine, I leaned down to remove a clump of hair from the drain. I couldn't see clearly because of the steam and dim light. It took the nerve endings in my skin a moment to process that the thing between my fingers was not strands of my brown hair but a giant cockroach. The roach's exoskeleton felt like plastic as it squirmed in my hand. I yelled *Fuuuuuck!,* dropped the roach, jumped out of the tub, and ran.

Roaches have been around since 300 million BC, way before the dinosaurs. And humans have been disgusted by them since we had ways to document our disgust. Three thousand years ago, the Egyptian Book of the Dead included a spell to eradicate roaches. In the novel by Brazilian writer Clarice Lispector, *The Passion According to G.H.,* a wealthy artist enters her maid's stark white room, sees a cockroach, and spends the majority of the novel spiraling into an existential crisis. In Kafka's *Metamorphosis,* traveling salesman Gregor Samsa wakes up one morning from an anxious dream transformed into an insect—possibly a beetle, maybe a cockroach—and disgusts his entire family.

Roaches are mostly harmless, but they can make us very sick with salmonella—and on the rare occasion, kill us. Aside from the diseases it might carry, it is the cockroach's appearance that likely repels us most. Its greasy auburn body. Its long spindly antennae. Its hairy legs. The odor it emits, which causes food to taste bad and one's allergies to worsen. Its speed. A cockroach can run three miles per hour. Disgust has evolved in humans as a disease-avoidant behavior. Disgust is our brain attempting to protect us from harm.

2. With fear

In the Russian fairytale "The Giant Cockroach" by Korney Chukovsky, a cockroach enters the animal kingdom and is found to be so revolting that wolves eat each other out of fear. The cockroach ends up becoming the ruler of the kingdom. In the contested 2020 Belarusian election, brave protesters were seen holding up signs against the president also known as the last remaining European dictator, Alexander Lukashenko. The signs read "stop the cockroach." Lukashenko has been in power in my birthplace of Belarus since 1994.

The fear of cockroaches is called *Katsaridaphobia. Katsarida* is Greek for cockroach. It is speculated that *Katsaridaphobia* may be brought on by a home infestation or finding a cockroach in one's food. Due to colonialism and cargo ships, roaches are coterminous with human existence all over the modern world. Where there are humans, there are cockroaches. Yet, out of the 4,500 known species of roaches, only thirty are found in human habitats. The most common roach is the small German cockroach that has so completely adapted to living with humans that it cannot survive without us. Other species include the enormous American cockroach (originally from West Africa), better known by its publicist-approved name, the water bug. These roaches can even fly, albeit clumsily.

No one really liked my high school drama teacher. Mostly because she was too dictatorial, too militant. There was a lot of yelling when there probably should've been more trust falls and games of Zip Zap Zop. She later became a high school dean, which was clearly a better fit. I was afraid of her, of her dominance. Afraid of the shitty roles she would cast me in if she found out that I didn't like her. One night, during a rehearsal of *Harvey*—a play about kindness and friendship in which a rich drunk befriends a giant invisible white rabbit—my high school drama teacher suddenly jumped up from her folding chair and started flailing her limbs in all directions, gesticulating wildly. I had never seen her so animated, so vulnerable. She was screaming. "It fell down my shirt! It fell down my shirt!" "It" was a cockroach that had found its way to the ceiling of the auditorium and fallen thirty feet down her shirt. A statistical anomaly. We all stared, stunned into silence, grasping our shirt collars.

3. With compassion

The term "cockroaach" is a common racial slur. According to the Environment & Society Portal, the term "cockroach" was originally used to demean African slaves arriving in roach infested slave ships. During the Rwandan genocide, Hutu extremists called the Tutsi *inyenzi* which translates to "cockroaches." The slur has been thrown around more recently by politicians when discussing immigrants. The roach invokes infestation, uncleanness, poverty, disease, and reproduction and is seen by some as the perfect description of the feared migrant.

Experts agree that disgust is not only a biological trait but also a cultural one. We learn from society what to find disgusting. In the *Black Mirror* episode "Men Against Fire," a near future military operation gives soldiers a neural implant called MASS, meant to eliminate their compassion in the battlefield. Instead of seeing civilians as victims of war, the device turns these innocent people into inhuman monstrous "roaches." MASS allows the soldiers to commit heinous crimes without guilt. In the episode, the protagonist's MASS glitches, and he is shown the reality of his xenophobia and feels compassion. MASS is not science fiction but based on an actual drug regimen attempted by scientists during the Iraq War to enable soldiers to take part in war crimes without suffering PTSD.

When I was in my early twenties, I worked at a retail store in Santa Monica. I sold overpriced ballet flats to supermodels, Helen Mirren, and the woman who wrote the children's book *If You Give a Mouse a*

Cookie. I got the job because the store was managed by a gorgeous energetic Bulgarian girl. She loved that I was also Eastern European, and I wasn't bad at selling shoes. I became her assistant. The owners were a cruel posh British woman and her hot son. When the British woman was in town, she would make me her servant. I would buy her Mocha-Frappuccinos from Starbucks and bring her sandals to the nail salon. One day, when my Bulgarian manager and I were working on a holiday window display, I tripped over a shoe box. "Clumsy girl," the British woman berated me with pursed lips before continuing to list all the times I'd been clumsy until I couldn't take it anymore. I cried in the storage closet and left. All I could think about on the drive home was what my manager had told me the other day, how she had overheard the British woman refer to Eastern Europeans as the cockroaches of Europe. I'm sure it didn't help that I was also a Jew.

4. With respect

Cockroaches are survivors. They can live for over a month with their heads chopped off. They can survive on dead and decaying matter. They are cannibals, capable of eating their squished cousins when there's nothing else to forage. They can hold their breath for up to forty minutes. It has been rumored that they can survive a nuclear war and take over where humans left off. And while moss and flour beetles can handle more radiation than the common cockroach, roaches are still up there on the list of nuclear survivors. In fact, they have been seen thriving in the detritus of Chernobyl, crawling out of the rubble in Hiroshima. Chernobyl is only ten miles away from Belarus' southern border.

Once, I accidentally boiled a cockroach while steaming some clothes and watched its little legs squirm to life in the bowl of the steamer. In the realm of animal symbolism, the cockroach is associated with resilience and adaptation. They can crawl between the narrowest openings, through the darkest of sewers, and survive. What is disgusting about survival?

In *The Passion According to G.H.,* Lispetor muses, "The mystery of human destiny is that we are fated, but that we have the freedom to fulfill or not fulfill our fate: realization of our fated destiny depends on us. While inhuman beings like the cockroach realize the entire cycle without going astray because they make no choices."

Roaches played a big role in a complicated romance in my twenties. He would eventually become my ex. The score card was always pulled out during our fights, and we would stand there shamefully rehashing all the ways each had wronged the other. Before we moved in together, he lived in an apartment by the freeway on a dead-end street in Los Angeles' Chinatown. His neighbors were Chinese immigrants who played mahjong and ate dried fish and grew scallions outside. Sometimes my boyfriend would exchange his cardboard recycling for Chinese melon or leafy greens or "canned meat in juices." When we opened his front door and turned on the lights, a sea of small German cockroaches would scurry away in all directions. We didn't care much about the roaches, as we were too preoccupied with our long nights of drinking and arguing. One night, I was so pissed off that when an enormous cockroach scurried by my foot, I smashed it dramatically with my boot. I wanted it to die along with my unhappiness, but it lived and scurried away a little flatter but not yet dead.

5. With wonder

There is a story my uncle likes to tell about me as a baby in Belarus. How curious I was. How my parents and I lived above a pelmeni shop. How little we had but how we made the most of it. How when I learned to scoot and then crawl, I would chase the roaches. Uninhibited, I would try to catch them with my stubby baby fingers and make them my little friends.

After hearing this story, my writer-friend Olga told me about this nineteenth century Russian novel recently translated to English by Fiona Bell. It's called *The Talnikov Family* by the female writer Avdotya Panaeva. It's about a family in 1820's St. Petersburg. With little freedom, the children find small joys in playing with the household roaches, cutting out figurines from a deck of playing cards and gluing them to their backs so that when they would scurry the roaches would resemble a miniature army.

The famous song "La Cucaracha" dates from the time of the Mexican Revolution. The first verse translates as: "The cockroach, the cockroach, can't walk anymore because it doesn't have marijuana to smoke." The end of a joint, where the harshest last numb of weed lives, is called a roach. This term for a partially smoked joint likely first came from a *New Yorker* article about a writer at a 1930s marijuana party. You often cough after hitting a "roach." It's a big dry cough that is rumored to make the high stronger, to make it reach your brain faster, to glaze your eyes red, and to give you that funny floaty hungry cosmic feeling of wonder that only weed can offer.

After moving into a studio apartment, I went to war with roaches. They were the kind that flew and were unafraid to crawl on my bed to get away from me and my attempts to murder them. On a hot Los Angeles summer night after a teary phone conversation with my mama about the roaches and the ex and the pandemic and the yellow sky from nearby fires and the power going out because of rolling blackouts, I decided to take a bath. I lit some candles and hit a joint and pretended my new apartment wasn't infested with roaches. I hoped the bath could be a sort of baptism. But a roach found me in the bathtub. Before I could get up and lift my slipper to murder him, I felt that funny floaty feeling of wonder and began to laugh at the cosmic joke of it all. The roach stuck around watching me. Together, we survived.

September 2023

Contributor Bios

Stephanie Austin is the author of *Something I Might Say,* a CNF chapbook with WTAW Press. Her debut novel *Burn* is coming in 2026 with Cowboy Jamboree Press. Find more of her work at stephanieaustin.net or follow her on social media on Instagram (@stephanie.d.austin) or Bluesky (@stephanieaustin.bsky.social).

Andrew Bertaina is the author of the essay collection, *The Body Is A Temporary Gathering Place* (Autofocus 2024), the book-length essay, *Ethan Hawke & Me* (Barrelhouse, 2025), and the short-story collection, *One Person Away From You* (Moon City Press Award Winner 2021).

Aaron Burch is the author of A *Kind of In-Between* and *Year of the Buffalo,* among others, and the editor of *How to Write a Novel: An Anthology of 20 Craft Essays About Writing, None of Which Ever Mention Writing,* and the journals Short Story, Long and HAD. His next book, *Tacoma,* is coming from Autofocus Books in 2026. He's online lots of places, including here: www.aaronburch.net.

Teresa Carmody (she/they) is a writer of fiction, creative nonfiction, interarts collaborations, and hybrid forms. Her books include *A Healthy Interest in the Lives of Others* (2025), *The Reconception of Marie* (2020), *Maison Femme: a fiction* (2015), and *Requiem* (2005). Their writing has appeared in *LitHub, Los Angeles Review of Books, Michigan Quarterly Review, Matters of Feminist Practice, WaterStone Review, Lifework,* and elsewhere. A co-founding director of Les Figues Press in Los Angeles, Carmody co-edited *I'll Drown My Book: Conceptual Writing by Women* and *TrenchArt Monograph: hurry up please its time.* She currently lives in Omaha and teaches in the Writer's Workshop and low-residency MFA in Creative Writing Program at University of Nebraska Omaha. Find Carmody on Instagram @troseistrose and online at teresacarmody.com.

Danielle Chelosky is a writer and journalist from New York. She is the author of *Pregaming Grief.*

Thad DeVassie is a writer and artist/painter from Ohio. He is the author of three chapbooks and has a novelette-in-flash arriving in 2026. Find more of his work at www.thaddevassie.com.

Chance Dibben is a writer, photographer, music-maker, and former comedian based in Lawrence, KS. His poems and shorts have appeared in *Split Lip, Reality Beach, Horsethief, Yes Poetry, Atlas and Alice, matchbook,* among others. Together with Melissa Fite Johnson, he co-hosts VOLTA, a reading and open mic series. His ambient/noise/drone project, SELVEDGE, has earned positive recognition, including features in Bandcamp's monthly Best Experimental and Best Ambient Music columns. Learn more at chancedibben.com.

Erin Dorney is a poet based in Western New York. She is the author of *Yes I Am Human I Know You Were Wondering* (Autofocus, March 2025), *The Usual Arteries* (Illuminated Press), *Grating, Darling, Full of Dirt* (Common Meter Press), *I Am Not Famous Anymore: Poems After Shia LaBeouf* (Mason Jar Press), and many zines. Erin's writing has been published in *Autofocus, Tolka, HAD,* and other literary journals. Her literary artwork and installations have been featured at the Center for Maine Contemporary Art, the Minnesota Center for Book Arts, and Susquehanna Art Museum. Learn more at www.erindorney.com.

Suzy Eynon is the author of the prose chapbooks *Commuting*, from the Ghost City Press summer series, and *Being Seen*, forthcoming from Ethel. Her writing has appeared in *jmww, Roanoke Review, Passages North, South Dakota Review, X-R-A-Y,* and elsewhere. She grew up in Arizona and lives in Seattle. Connect online at suzyeynon.com.

Cameron Gearen's full-length collection, *Some Perfect Year,* came out from Shearsman Press in 2016. In 2023, Seven Kitchens Press published her chapbook, *Sorry, Wept the Littered Riverbed.* Her essays and poems have appeared in *The Washington Post, Hippocampus, Pithead Chapel, Dame Magazine, The Antioch Review, Green Mountains Review, Fence, River Styx, Full Grown People*, and many other journals. She has benefited from a Barbara Deming Money for Women grant. Former US Poet Laureate Robert Pinsky selected her first chapbook for publication. She was the Hemingway Writer-in-Residence at Hemingway's birth home in Oak Park, Illinois, from 2017-2019. She lives in River Forest, Illinois, and runs her own business as an educational consultant.

Kaycie Hall is a writer and translator living in New York City by way of Jackson, MS.

Lyd Havens is the author of the chapbook *Chokecherry (*Game Over Books, 2021) and a co-author of *I Wish I Wasn't Royalty: A Playable Chapbook* (Game Over Books, 2020). Her work has previously been published in *Ploughshares, Poetry Northwest,* and *New Delta Review,* among others. Lyd is currently earning an MFA in poetry from the University of Virginia. She lives in Charlottesville with her fiancé and a tree full of red-breasted robins.

WA Hawkins is a writer and journalist in New Orleans. You can find his work on *NPR, The Guardian, Scalawag Magazine, Rejection Letters, HAD,* and elsewhere.

Kiyanna Hill is a left-handed Black poet. Her work has been featured or forthcoming from *Honey Literary, The Maine Review, Vagabond City,* and *Cream City Review.* She is a Ph.D student at Georgia State University and poetry co-editor of *Beyond Bars,* a journal of literature and art that publishes the work of those affected by the carceral system.

Claire Hopple is the author of six books. Her stories have appeared in *Southwest Review, Forever Mag, Wigleaf, Cleveland Review of Books,* and others. More at clairehopple.com.

Lexi Kent-Monning is the author of the novel *The Burden of Joy.* She's an alumna of the Tyrant Books workshop Mors Tua Vita Mea in Sezze Romano, Italy, and was awarded a residency at Ghost Ranch in Abiquiu, New Mexico. Her writing has been published in *The Believer, Los Angeles Review of Books, Paste, Joyland, Little Engines,* and elsewhere. She lives in Los Angeles.

Beth Kephart, a National Book Award finalist, is the award-winning author of some three-dozen books in multiple genres, including, most recently *Wife | Daughter | Self: A Memoir in Essays, My Life in Paper: Adventures in Ephemera*, and *Tomorrow Will Bring Sunday's News: A Philadelphia Story.* She is a paper artist and can be found at bethkephartbooks.com and The Hush and the Howl, her substack.

Jillian Luft is a Florida writer. Her first book, *Scumbag Summer,* was published by House of Vlad Press. She's currently working on a memoir about caretaking for a terminally ill mother as a teen. You can read more of her writing at jillianluft.com.

Amy Lyons has had writing in *Waxwing, Rose Books Reader Vol. 1, BULL, Rejection Letters, HAD, Best Microfictions, The Independent, LA Weekly,* and more. Her work has been supported by grants and residencies from Millay Colony, Vermont Studio Center, and Mid Atlantic Arts Foundation. She holds an MFA from Bennington.

Kirsti MacKenzie (@KeersteeMack) is a writer and editor in chief of *Major 7th Magazine*. Her debut novel, *Better to Beg,* will be released with Sweet Trash Press/House of Vlad in Fall 2025. You can find the rest of her work at kirstimackenzie.com.

Kristine Langley Mahler is the author of three nonfiction books, A *Calendar Is a Snakeskin, Curing Season: Artifacts,* and *Teen Queen Training* (forthcoming with Autofocus, 2026). Her work has been supported by the Nebraska Arts Council and Art at Cedar Point and twice named Notable in *Best American Essays.* A memoirist experimenting with the truth on the suburban prairie, Kristine makes her home outside Omaha, Nebraska. She is the director of Split/Lip Press.

Kevin Maloney is the author of *The Red-Headed Pilgrim* (Two Dollar Radio, Jan 2023), *Horse Girl Fever* (CLASH Books, Jan 2025), and *Cult of Loretta* (Lazy Fascist, 2015).

Mike Nagel is the author of *Duplex* and *Culdesac,* both from Autofocus Books. He lives in Plano, Texas.

Abigail Oswald writes about art, fame, and connection. Her work has appeared in places like *Best Microfiction, Bright Wall/Dark Room, DIAGRAM, Memoir Mixtapes, The Rumpus,* and a memory vending machine. She's also the author of *Microfascination,* a newsletter on pop culture rabbit holes. Abigail holds an MFA from Sarah Lawrence College and can be found at the movie theater in at least one parallel universe at any given time. More online at abigailwashere.com.

Holly Pelesky writes essays, fiction and poetry. She has an MFA and an MLIS from midwestern institutions. Her prose can be found in *CutBank, Vol.1 Brooklyn, Chautauqua,* other places. Her collection of letters to her daughter, *Cleave,* was published by Autofocus Books. She works as a librarian and a writing center consultant while raising boys in Omaha. Last year, her daughter moved in with them for a brief and gorgeous time.

Nina Perlman is a writer, photographer, and photo editor born and raised in New York City. She received her MFA from Image Text Ithaca. In addition to *Autofocus Lit,* her writing has been featured in *DIAGRAM, Write or Die Magazine, Spectra,* and *Soft Union.* She also writes a newsletter on Substack called *[A Scaffold].*

Abigail Richards is a queer writer and artist living in Toronto, Canada. Her work has been featured in various literary publications. You can find more at abigailrichards.ca.

Erin Riedel is a writer and therapist living in Louisville, KY. Her work has appeared in *Taco Bell Quarterly, Bullshit Lit,* and elsewhere. Her many loves include Boston terriers, barbershop harmony, and old Volvos. Visit her online at www.erinriedel.com.

D.T. Robbins is the author of books like *Birds Aren't Real* and *Leasing*. He's the founding editor of *Rejection Letters*.

Paul Rousseau is a disabled writer and author of *Friendly Fire: A Fractured Memoir*. His work has appeared in *Newsweek, Catapult, Wigleaf, SmokeLong Quarterly*, and Roxane Gay's *The Audacity*, among others, and has been selected for Best Small Fictions 2024, the Wigleaf Top 50, as well as nominated for a Pushcart Prize, Best of the Net, and Best American Science Fiction & Fantasy. You can read his stories and essays at Paul-Rousseau.com.

Diana Ruzova is a Soviet-born writer based in Los Angeles. She has an MFA in literature and creative nonfiction from the Bennington Writing Seminars. In summer 2024, she was a Kenyon Review Writers Workshop Fellow. Her interviews, essays, articles, and criticism have appeared in the *Los Angeles Times, Los Angeles Review of Books, BOMB, Flaunt, Hyperallergic, New York Magazine's The Cut*, and other publications. You can read more of Diana's writing at dianaruzova.com.

Zach Savich's latest books are the poetry collection *Momently* (Black Ocean, 2024) and the critical-memoir-for-performance *A Field of Telephones* (53rd State Press, 2025). He is a recipient of fellowships from the National Endowment for the Arts, the Vermont Studio Center, and elsewhere. Recent work appears in journals including *Chicago Review, Iowa Review*, and *Puerto del Sol*. Savich teaches at the Cleveland Institute of Art.

David Schuman's fiction and nonfiction has been published in *Fence, Joyland, Missouri Review, Conjunctions*, and other magazines, and anthologized in the Pushcart Prize Anthology and other anthologies. His prose chapbook, *Best Men*, is published by Tammy Press. He teaches and directs the writing program at Washington University in St. Louis.

David Shields is the internationally bestselling author of twenty-five books, including *Reality Hunger* (which, in 2020, Lit Hub named one of the most important books of the past decade), *The Thing About Life Is That One Day You'll Be Dead* (New York Times bestseller), *Black Planet: Facing Race During an NBA Season* (finalist for the National Book Critics Circle Award and PEN USA Award), *Remote: Reflections on Life in the Shadow of Celebrity* (PEN/Revson Award), and *Other People: Takes & Mistakes* (NYTBR Editors' Choice). *The Very Last Interview* was published by New York Review Books in 2022.

Erin Slaughter is the author of the short story collection *A Manual for How to Love Us* (Harper Perennial, 2023), and two books of poetry: *The Sorrow Festival* (CLASH Books, 2022), and *I Will Tell This Story to the Sun Until You Remember That You Are the Sun* (New Rivers Press, 2019). Her debut memoir, *The Dead Dad Diaries,* is forthcoming from Autofocus Books in 2025. Her writing has appeared in *Lit Hub, Electric Literature, CRAFT, The Georgia Review,* and elsewhere. She is currently Assistant Professor of Creative Writing at Coastal Carolina University. Find her online at erin-slaughter.com.

Sabrina Small lives in the Berlin neighbourhood of Wedding with her two daughters where she runs the quirky store Found in Wedding, which hosts writing events. In addition to publishing autofiction and hosting the literary podcast *Self Exposure*, Sabrina is also an interior designer and antique dealer. It's exhausting, but there's an existential void waiting to crush her if she ever slows down.

Brianna Snow lives in big cities and writes small stories. Her work appears in the anthologies *To Carry Her Home, Sleep Is a Beautiful Colour,* and *Fuel: Prize-Winning Flash Fictions Raising Funds to Fight Fuel Poverty.*

Andrew Sottile lives on the Connecticut coast with his wife and son.

Christy Tending (she/they) is the author of *High Priestess of the Apocalypse.* Their work has been published in *Longreads, The Rumpus,* and *Electric Literature,* and received a notable mention in *Best American Science and Nature Writing 2023.* They are the recipient of a residency at Yaddo and the Birdcoat

Editors' Prize in the Essay 2024. They live in Oakland, California with their family. You can learn more about their work at www.christytending.com.

Laurie Rachkus Uttich is the author of the poetry collection, *Somewhere, a Woman Lowers the Hem of Her Skirt* (Riot In Your Throat, 2022). Her essays and poetry have been published in *Brevity; Creative Nonfiction; Poets and Writers; Rattle; River Teeth; Ruminate; Speculative Nonfiction; Split Lip Magazine; The Sun; Sweet: A Literary Confection;* and others. She teaches at the University of Central Florida and leads creative writing workshops at a maximum-security correctional center for men in Orlando.

Donna Vorreyer is the author of *Unrivered* (forthcoming, 2025), *To Everything There Is* (2020), *Every Love Story is an Apocalypse Story* (2016) and *A House of Many Windows* (2013), all from Sundress Publications. She hosts the monthly online reading series A Hundred Pitchers of Honey and is a co-founder/editor of the new journal *Asterales: A Journal of Arts & Letters.*

Alyson Zetta Williams is a writer from Los Angeles. Read her stuff at sorry4444.substack.com and @alysonzw.

Lena Ziegler is a multi-genre writer with a special interest in hybrid work. Her writing has appeared in *Split Lip Magazine, Indiana Review, Literary Orphans, Miracle Monocle, Duende, Dream Pop Press, Anti-Heroin Chic, Gambling the Aisle* and others. She is a co-founder of the literary journal and press *The Hunger.* She holds an MFA from Western Kentucky University and a PhD from Bowling Green State University. She lives in Pennsylvania with her husband. You can find her online at www.lenaziegler.com.

Acknowledgments

The following works were included in the following books after publication in *Autofocus Lit* and before publication of this anthology:

"A Field of Telephones" by Zach Savich
in *A Field of Telephones* (53rd Street Press, 2025)

"Childhood" by David Shields
in *The Very Last Interview* (NYRB, 2022)

"The Nurse's Lament" by Lexi Kent-Monning
in *The Burden of Joy* (Rejection Letters Press, 2023)

"About Accidental Firearm Discharge on Campus" by Paul Rousseau
in *Friendly Fire: A Fractured Memoir* (Harper Horizon, 2024)

"Kill Floor" by Stephanie Austin
in *Something I Might Say (WTAW Press, 2023)*

"Say You're Pregnant" by Holly Pelesky
in *Cleave* (Autofocus Books, 2022)

"Unvanishing" by Beth Kephart
in *My Life in Paper* as "Blank Book" (Temple University Press, 2023)

Thank you to Ryan Skaryd, Sheila Mulrooney, Erin Slaughter, Kaycie Hall, Sienna Zeilinger. Brian Salmons, Alo Devine, Marin Sardy, Joanna Lyons-Little, James Roach, Kakie Pate, Nathan Xie, Tim States, Mike Nagel, Steven Arcieri, Kika Win Ling, John Comerci, Charika Swanepoel, Christina Kellagher, Sarah Olive, and anyone else who read (or edited!) for the journal at any point and who I'm forgetting now because memory fails and I was bad at keeping records.

Thank you to the included writers. Thank you to the unincluded.

About the Editor

Michael Wheaton is the author of the essay *Home Movies* (Bunny Presse, 2024). His writing has appeared previously online in *Essay Daily, Diagram, Cleveland Review of Books, HAD, Rejection Letters,* and elsewhere. He edits and publishes Autofocus Books. From 2020-2024, he produced and hosted *The Lives of Writers* podcast and edited and published the online journal *Autofocus Lit.* More at mwheaton.net.

also from Autofocus Books

Duplex — Mike Nagel

XO — Sara Rauch

Until It Feels Right — Emily Costa

Cleave — Holly Pelesky

Nextdoor in Colonialtown — Ryan Rivas

Too Much Tongue — Adrienne Marie Barrios & Leigh Chadwick

Picture Window — Danny Caine

the nature machine! — Tyler Gillespie

A Kind of In-Between — Aaron Burch

How to Write a Novel: An Anthology of 20 Craft Essays About Writing, None of Which Ever Mention Writing — ed. Aaron Burch

Hiraeth — Mistie Watkins

That Spell — Tate N. Oquendo

My Modest Blindness — Russell Brakefield

A Calendar Is A Snakeskin — Kristine Langley Mahler

Culdesac — Mike Nagel

Razed by TV Sets — Jason McCall

In the Away Time — Kristen E. Nelson

The Body Is A Temporary Gathering Place — Andrew Bertaina

Daughterhood — Emily Adrian

A Healthy Interest in the Lives of Others — Teresa Carmody

Leave: A Postpartum Account — Shayne Terry

Yes I Am Human I Know You Were Wondering — Erin Dorney

Organic Matter — E.N. Couturier

Out There in the Dark — Katharine Coldiron

Marginalia — Naomi Washer

A Revisionist History of Loving Men — Lena Ziegler

The Dead Dad Diaries — Erin Slaughter

www.ingramcontent.com/pod-product-compliance
Lightning Source LLC
LaVergne TN
LVHW091135080826
845145LV00008B/2162